Servant Leadership from the Middle

The Servant Leadership Series

Series Editor: Dr. Richard Kyte, Director of the
D. B. Reinhart Institute for Ethics in Leadership and Endowed
Professor of Ethics at Viterbo University

What Is Servant Leadership?

Servant leadership stems from the conviction that the best leaders are those who have a deep personal commitment to the common good—that is, to the well-being of all and not just a few—and out of that commitment comes the desire to lead. What this means is that good leadership cannot be defined merely in terms of principles, techniques, or strategies; it is primarily a matter of character, originating in love and culminating in effective action. The foundational insight of servant leadership is that all leadership, properly understood, is an exercise of virtue and can be evaluated according to whether it leads to a flourishing life for individuals and communities. The practice of servant leadership seeks to inspire and engage people to work for the greater good every day.

The D. B Reinhart Institute for Ethics in Leadership

Since 1999, the D. B. Reinhart Institute for Ethics in Leadership at Viterbo University has brought people together in fruitful conversation about ethical ideas and issues, inspiring people to lead ethical lives while at the same time helping to develop leadership abilities to further the common good in communities and organizations.

Servant Leadership from the Middle

By
Bernard L. Osborne

Fulcrum Publishing
Wheat Ridge, Colorado

Library of Congress Cataloging-in-Publication Data

Names: Osborne, Bernard L., author.
Title: Servant leadership from the middle / by Bernard L. Osborne.
Description: Wheat Ridge, Colorado : Fulcrum Publishing, [2022] |
Includes
  bibliographical references.
Identifiers: LCCN 2022010520 | ISBN 9781682753385 (paperback)
Subjects: LCSH: Servant leadership.
Classification: LCC HM1261 .O83 2022 | DDC 658.4/092--dc23/
eng/20220310
LC record available at https://lccn.loc.gov/2022010520

Printed in the United States
0 9 8 7 6 5 4 3 2 1

Fulcrum Publishing
3970 Youngfield Street, Wheat Ridge, Colorado 80033
(800) 992-2908 • (303) 277-1623
www.fulcrumbooks.com

To Mom and Dad

Contents

"Faith dare the soul to go further than it can see."

—William Clark

Foreword

The most common question I get from adult students is how to deal with a bad supervisor. The question rarely comes during class. It comes during a break or in a conversation after class. They don't want to ask the question in front of others.

But they are not alone. Most workers suffer under poor leadership of some sort. If they did not, employee engagement would be much higher than it is.

Being a good supervisor is not easy. Many employees are given some limited supervisory responsibilities relatively early in their careers, usually with no experience and little to no training. What's more, some companies make it down-right difficult to be a good leader when one is operating from the middle.

I had a conversation once with a factory manager who had just been chewed out by his boss. The problem? The manager wasn't "staying in his lane." The employees he supervised felt respected and empowered. When employees from other parts of the company heard about this, they began coming to him for advice. Trying to be a good leader had made him stand out—admired by those on the factory floor, suspected by his peers in management.

This is not an unusual dilemma for managers: Is it better to stand out or to fit in? The answer, of course, depends on what kind of person one wants to be, how one wants to face life.

Bernard Osborne has written about his experience of learning to lead by facing deliberately upward and outward, in the direction of growth. This is every person's natural orientation, until resistance in its various forms pushes back, stunting our aspirations and forcing our attention downward and inward. "Go along to get along" becomes the unspoken mantra of too many unfortunate souls who never push through to their full potential.

A few of those who do push through may reach the top. When they write books about their experience they too often forget the doubts and uncertainties they struggled to over-come in the middle period of their lives. That's understandable, because leadership at the top of an organization not only looks very different from leadership in the middle, if *feels* very differ-ent. There is much less resistance in giving orders downward than giving suggestions upward.

There are approximately 39,000 chief executive offi-cers in the United States and an estimated 8 million managers (counting only large firms). There are millions more who have some sort of supervisory responsibilities. In other words, the vast majority of employees with some kind of leadership role in organizations are operating from the middle. They remain in the middle for the rest of their careers, and their influence on the well-being of their respective organizations is significantly underrated.

Gallup estimates that 70 percent of the variance in employee engagement scores within companies is due to managers. And yet, more often than not (82 percent of the time), companies select the wrong people to fill those roles. Why is that? Mainly, I think, because we are still beholden to a false distinction between managing and leading. Since we don't expect managers to be leaders, we don't look for the right traits in the people we choose to fill those roles, and we don't provide them with the right kind of guidance to develop into good leaders.

Everybody who takes on a leadership role wants to be a good leader. They want to be effective, to be a positive influence, but too often they do not know how. Many think real leadership has to wait until the next step up the ladder. They say to themselves: it's something I can do in the future, when my career has advanced, when I get promoted, when I get that new job with more responsibility, more power.

But good leadership isn't about power; it's about attitude. It's about looking upward and outward, about stretching and growing, learning and reflecting. Good leadership starts with an inward journey and culminates in outward influence.

Osborne reminds us that the best path when leading from the middle is to commit to the growth of others through the effects of positive influence. It is a kind of leadership that does not neatly correspond to organizational charts. It refuses to stay in its lane. It operates through the careful cultivation of trust and good will. It enriches the lives of those who commit to it and the lives of all those it touches.

Richard Kyte

March 10, 2022

Preface

Before I began writing this book, I did a Google search of "books on leadership." Google returned 809,000,000 results in 1.05 seconds. Knowing this, you might ask yourself, why would anyone decide to write another book on leadership in an already oversaturated market? Or you might ask yourself, why should I, a new and emerging leader, use my precious spare time to read another book on leadership when so many have already been written by intelligent, accomplished, and proven leaders?

When most people think of successful leaders they typically think of a CEO, entrepreneur, college professor, philosopher, leadership coach, military officer, or a person high up in a hierarchy pyramid; someone in a position of power. Many of these people have in fact already written books on their leadership journey, sharing their profound wisdom and life experiences, and many have influenced not only my own leadership journey but those of countless others. With that said, I did not write this book pretending to be on their level or to compete with them. Instead, this book is sincerely written for those who I believe will benefit the most. It is written for those brave souls who have, or may decide to take the scary, uncertain, but noble and fulfilling first step up and out into a leadership position.

I wrote this book for you because I myself have walked in the shoes of a new and emerging leader. Wherever you are in your new leadership journey, whatever you are thinking, doubting, questioning, or stressed out about, we most likely have shared that experience. And just like you right now, I was left to figure it out on my own. Therefore, I would like to share with you the many lessons I have learned in my life of standing in the middle of the leadership road. With management demands coming from one direction and employee demands coming from the other, it's not always easy to balance yourself to stand and walk on that center line safely and successfully.

This book is not intended to be a source of easy answers, or a "just do this and say that when this happens" guide. It is instead a book of my experiences and reflections; one that I wish I would have had access to when I began my leadership journey. I can only approach this with hope (hope meaning confidence in the future) that this book will provide you with a new perspective, a clearer path, and a renewed purpose to help you with the daily struggles, conflicts, and the uncertain realities and challenges that come with being a new and emerging leader.

Throughout history, as new leaders faced these challenges, personal experience and mentoring by knowledgeable and caring mentors have always been the most effective teachers. In addition, and to our benefit, there are many leaders held in high regard throughout recorded history that we can learn from and model ourselves after. But regardless of this amount of information and past experience, an interesting shift in leadership training occurred in 1970s American society.

At this time organizations were taking for granted and abusing the spoils of a selfish and wasteful industrialized nation. This resulted in organizations failing to appreciate their employees. The ignorance of overproduction combined with elevated profits allowed organizations to adopt command-and-control management styles—authoritative and top-down—simply because they could afford to get away with it. Ultimately, the negative effects of this type of leadership not only forced organizations to adjust their frame of reference and mindset to find ways to better lead people, but they also had to increase employee and customer satisfaction to remain competitive on a global level.

Therefore, the leadership-training industry was born. Leadership training became the Band-Aid to help bail out and improve organizations. The intent of this training was to transform organizational leaders who had become dependent on the command-and-control management style with the many new theoretical and categorized leadership styles that were being born from, and because of it. The leadership-teaching bubble soon grew and eventually burst into the multibillion-dollar leadership-development industry we have today. Add into this the abundance of social media outlets, and it is apparent that anyone with time and an internet connection is now vying for your attention and offering their opinions of what leadership is or should be.

At this point, let me play the devil's advocate. With all the research, knowledge, and experience acquired and studied from decades and centuries of leadership history, with the creation of leadership theories, consultants, management associations, and online independents teaching and preaching leadership, why do we still have a worldwide leadership crisis today? Why have these Herculean efforts of thought and good intentions only produced more theories instead of widespread positive effects? Why is there still a struggle to motivate and engage civilians, workers, and organizations, to increase both employee, organizational, and customer satisfaction? In short, where are all the good leaders? Why has our production-driven mindset failed to mass-produce good leaders?

I believe it is because leadership theories are created from cultural, political, and societal factors, as well as other specific needs around the time and/or place of their creation. The leadership flood that began in the late 1970s, which is still flooding our world today, has the underlying intention and purpose of manufacturing leaders instead of growing them over time. The leadership training programs I have participated in were taught by caring instructors, and I believe those instructors had the best of intentions. Yet looking back on the curriculum now, I understand why I did not get what I needed from them.

Students are given a specific time period of training to "get it," and, regardless of whether we got "it," everyone would graduate from the programs. I also observed senior leaders who participated in these programs who believed they were beyond the leadership training. Even though they attended the classes, they silently declared through their body language that they were above additional leadership education, and their auras had a negative influence on the rest of the participants—particularly for those employees who really needed comradery and guidance from them in this area in the most desperate of ways.

And when all was said and done we were sent away with our graduation certificates that declared we were now knowledgeable enough to go back into the workplace and successfully use and apply our newly acquired education. And just like most people who graduate from high school, once that diploma was received they never looked back or reflected on the curriculum or experience. That piece of paper became the document that signified the end of that chapter in life, and this is where I would always find myself after attending leadership programs.

Although I would at first be excited to attend these trainings, that feeling quickly dissipated because of the pressure of getting behind in my work duties while there. My thoughts were more concerned about what was going on at work and what I would have to do to catch up the next day. Therefore, I struggled to give my full attention to the curriculum, and would only apply enough of myself and my attention to complete the course. Just like what happens so often in many organizations, it does not matter how the jobs get done, only that it gets done. Too often this is what drives leadership training, and too often, these outcomes produce more interference with progress than they prevent.

After the course was completed and I was back at work, the certificate and study materials soon disappeared into a file cabinet or flash drive, and the trinkets handed out as reminders of the curriculum found their way to a shelf just like the knickknacks in your home—rarely looked at or thought of, just sitting there gathering dust. In the end, all the leadership theories I read and all the leadership programs I attended were not satisfying what I was yearning for inside. I knew there had to be a different and better way to lead people, but I lacked the articulation and community to bring forth the change I desired. Therefore I remained in a sort of leadership stasis for many years.

Since that time I have learned that leaders need to be grown, to be tended to, and not manufactured. The day I discovered Robert Greenleaf and servant leadership was the catalyst that gave meaning to my struggle. It provided direction and supplied a philosophy behind what I longed for and knew internally to be just and right. It is from this perspective that I decided to write this book and bring the Google search result to 809,000,001. It was from this inner drive and instinct that *Servant Leadership from the Middle* was born.

Now, a bit about servant leadership. The name "servant leader" in itself is an oxymoron, and it makes you think a bit more deeply about it. For example, how can a servant be a leader, how can a leader be a servant, how can one be both, and both be one? At this point you might be wondering what exactly servant leadership is. There are many definitions, and they all vary in uniqueness because servant leadership is understood, interpreted, and practiced differently by each person because of their unique life experiences. In fact, there are books dedicated to defining the philosophy. So, for me to try and offer a one-size-fits-all definition at this point would be in vain.

Therefore, I recommend reading the first book I read on the subject, *Insights on Leadership* by Larry Spears (1998). In it, Spears "identifies a set of ten characteristics . . . central to the development of servant-leaders" (p. 3), which are "listening, empathy, healing, awareness, persuasion, conceptualization, foresight, stewardship, commitment to the growth of people, and building community" (pp. 4–6). As a new and emerging leader, do not approach these characteristics as goals to be accomplished, or traits to be mastered but rather as guidelines and tools that you can use to help serve others and create positive change. Take what you learn and use your unique gifts and talents to make the world a better place, because *that* is the goal of servant leadership, and the true means to our ends.

For me, servant leadership is more a philosophy for living life rather than an applied theory of leadership. Greenleaf's philosophy helped me to find and discover strengths in myself that guided me in my leadership journey. It provided me the opportunity and resources to uncover and overcome personal biases; some of which I did not know I had. Servant leadership helped me gain new perspectives to improve personally as a new and emerging leader that also enhanced my leadership and relations with others. It helped me to incorporate reflection and contemplation into my thought process and life; something that is difficult to do in our fast-paced world today.

As a result, servant leadership has changed my life for the positive, not only at work but in all aspects, including family and community. I learned that leadership is not static, it is not theory to be learned, a certificate to be signed off on, information that is quickly forgotten in a drawer, or trinkets left gathering dust on a shelf. Servant leadership is the lifelong journey of learning and discovery, not only about yourself, but including and finding the good in others to raise them up and grow them positively whenever possible.

After learning more about Greenleaf and servant leadership, I discovered that even though cultural, political, and societal factors may always be changing, people, their basic needs, and human nature remain constant factors no matter what era or situations we may find ourselves in. Just like you cannot make the weekends or holidays come any faster, rush the growing of a tree or a crop on a farm, servant leadership relies, respects, and works with the natural growth cycle and well-being of human beings. The following chapters and life and leadership moments, from my perspective, are titled and reflect the life cycle of a tree; a life-form that continues to grow throughout its lifetime.

As McDonald's founder Ray Kroc said many years ago, you can either be "green and growing or ripe and rotting." Life and leadership are no different. We should always be concerned with continuous growth and self-development to better help and serve those around us. Continuous growth and development is the starting point, basis, and conclusion of the leadership growth cycle. I use the analogy of a tree's growth cycle because of its similarities to the stages of human growth. Trees, like humans, have four stages of growth: seedling (infancy), primary growth (childhood), secondary growth (adolescence), maturity (adulthood). Another similarity is that when trees reach their maximum height in their primary stage, they then begin to grow outward.

Trees, like humans, reach their maximum height by their secondary growth stage. And it is at this stage that humans are able to grow into maturity through education, experience, and reflection. Servant leaders are dedicated and devoted to growing more leaders, and to provide the right conditions for growth by taking care of the grounds in which life can grow. And like a path through an arboretum it can serve as a bridge over water, not only showing where you are now, and taking you where you want to go, but also resembling the twists and turns of the uncertain leadership path we are all on. This book represents my leadership journey, as I progressed on my path through the stages of growth, and into my uncertain leadership journey that continues to this day.

In chapter 1, "Seedling," I talk about my backstory and early experiences in the world of work, and how these experiences were setting me up on the path to servant leadership. Chapter 2, "Primary Growth," begins with a couple of short stories relating the craziness of the world and workplace, and then dives deeper into my leadership beginnings. I share a personal story of how empathy became a major influence in my work and life, and how honest self-reflection set me further on the path toward servant leadership, which eventually led to my first real encounter with it, where I witnessed its power to create community, social bonding, and social bridging. Chapter 3, "Secondary Growth," focuses on advice for introducing, applying, and being a servant leader in your organization. There are two "subchapters"—the first helps you understand the organization and focuses on assessment, social capital and trust, communication, motivation, and engagement. The second subchapter is on understanding the self, which focuses on the power of the ego, and dives further into reflection. Chapter 4, "Maturity," ties it all together and provides an example of how personal growth and leadership is grown organically through self-reflection and contemplation.

Throughout the book I offer my perspective and personal experiences by sharing what I call life and leadership moments, and the first *life and leadership moment comes right now: the only advice I will offer you is that successful leadership always starts with the heart.* The rest of the book is now yours to take and apply, or discard, as you and your situation see fit. Just like how I use the analogy of a tree to describe human growth, I like the analogy of a leadership "arboretum" to describe leadership as it relates to work, family, and community. For instance, all life on earth will only grow as well as conditions permit. Each individual species of life has its own unique requirements for growth, and all require basic and fundamental elements in different amounts and combinations before the magic of growth can happen.

The servant leader's vocation is to figure out and provide the conditions required for each unique life to achieve maximum growth and sustainability. Leaders are like farmers, and there are two types. There is the self-serving leader, who takes from the land and gives nothing back, and there is the servant leader who respects the land and works with it to keep it rich and fertile. Your home, work, and community are the land, its people are the seeds, and you are the new and emerging servant leader. May your harvests be as plentiful as your sowing. I welcome you to walk with me now through the leadership arboretum.

CHAPTER 1

Seedling

This first stage of growth is to realize we are born with compassion and empathy for others, and the ability to be true to them and ourselves.

I began my entry into the adult world of work when I was thirteen and fourteen years old. During summer vacations my parents sent me on an airplane from Racine, Wisconsin, to Rockville, Maryland, to stay with my sister and brother-in-law. This is where and when I learned to have compassion and empathy for others, and the ability to be true to myself; both, as I would discover, are components of servant leadership. My brother-in-law owned and operated a gas station, and I was fortunate enough to be employed by him as a "pump jockey." During the 1980s, pump jockeys worked outside at the gas pumps and monitored the self-service and full-service sides of the gas pumps.

On the self-service side, I was responsible for ensuring that everyone who pumped their own gas paid for it. This meant that I, a thirteen-year-old kid, had the responsibility of having a large fold of paper bills in my right-front pocket, and a coin change dispenser attached to my belt on the left to give out change for customer transactions. During the morning and evening rush hours there were always long lines of cars waiting for gas, and if I let a customer leave without paying for their gas it meant that that transaction would come out of my paycheck. This reality in itself guaranteed I paid close attention, as excuses were costly and not tolerated.

Credit cards were in their infancy then. Electronic payment was not an option. Instead, to charge a credit card, the pump jockey had to place the customer's card into a small rectangular device where a carbon-copy form was placed over it. The device had a hand roller that transferred the card's information from its raised characters onto the form that created the receipts.

On the full-service side, customers would drive up to the pumps, roll down their window, and tell the pump jockey to either "fill 'er up" or dispense the customer's desired dollar amount of gas while the customer remained in the car. Other amenities of full service were cleaning the windows, checking and topping off the car's fluids, and checking tire pressure and adding air if needed. (I always dreaded the customer on a hot summer day who would insist I check their car's radiator fluid. This was a dangerous and unnecessary job, and, yes, there were people who would insist that a thirteen-year-old kid open up a piping-hot radiator cap.)

I learned many valuable lessons during those summer days. First, my young teenage eyes got the impression that the

East Coast had a more competitive lifestyle than my "Midwest-nice" upbringing. But what I also discovered from the interactions with those competitive East Coast customers was that people's basic needs are still the same regardless of a differences in their attitudes, opinions, or accents. I learned the servant leadership quality of listening, not just with my ears, but also with my senses. I remember quite a few customers who were having a bad day, or were insolent to me during our transaction, and some would return later to apologize and thank me for being kind, patient, and forgiving. These moments of humility made the long, hot days inhaling gas fumes, exhaust fumes, and cigarette smoke somehow better and worth the paycheck.

The pump-jockey job provided my first taste of real responsibility, and it is where I believe my work ethic was first established. I learned what having a sense of urgency meant, how it helped the goals of a business, and its significant and positive effect on the customer—a characteristic that would follow me throughout my life. My brother-in-law was my first boss, and he provided me my first *life and leadership moment: tolerate no favoritism, treat others in a just and right way, and have the same expectations for all.* If I, or any employee screwed up, he let us know. As a result, I wanted to work hard to not let him, or myself down. (And being able to spend my paychecks on whatever I wanted was an additional benefit!)

This taste of adulthood flew with me back to Wisconsin. When I turned fifteen and a half I knew I would be eligible to get my driver's license soon. My parents agreed to let me use one of their cars to drive to school and work if I could pay for my own auto insurance and gas. So, I enrolled in a private driving school, and my mother helped me get a job at the nursing home where she worked as a physical therapist. I was hired as an aide to the nurses' aides and would work part-time during the evenings after school and full-time on the weekends.

My duties there were to sort, fold, and deliver the residents' clothes and keep their water pitchers filled with fresh water and ice. On the weekend day shift I would replace the residents' bedding after the nurses got the residents out of their beds. I did this for about six months until new management took over and eliminated my job. I was then fortunate enough to be offered a new position working in the kitchen. I worked on the tray line where I read nutrition cards that instructed how much and what type of food was to be dispensed on the residents' trays, and I would transport the tray carts of food to the residents' rooms and to the dining halls.

I would then serve the trays to the residents, work in the dining rooms, and sometimes feed residents who could not feed themselves. Afterward, I gathered the tray carts and returned them to the washroom where I stripped them and sent them through the dishwasher. I performed this job until I graduated from high school, and after I graduated, I was promoted to the full-time position of stockman for the kitchen. My new responsibilities were to receive the deliveries of food and distribute the food to the appropriate storerooms, read the menus for the next day, and stock the kitchen. The experiences I gained in this position added to and enhanced my understanding of working with people and developing myself.

For instance, one evening the nurses were short-staffed, and they asked me to help feed a resident. The man did not talk, though I don't remember if this was because he could not or he just did not want to. I began to feed him his meal, and he ate all his dinner very well. I opened his dessert of applesauce and began to spoon it into his mouth. I noticed that he was consuming the applesauce faster than his dinner, so I assumed he really liked it. But when I offered the last spoonful of applesauce I discovered he had been saving every bite in his mouth and not swallowing any of it, because he suddenly spewed the entire dessert into my face. This relates to a *life and leadership moment: when you sense or notice something is off or out of the norm, pay attention and deal with it as soon as possible. More often than not it is your signal that something may be building that can blow up on you if it is not addressed in the early stages.*

The majority of residents never left the facility, and only a select and lucky few had family visit on a regular basis, so many of the residents were yearning for acknowledgment, connection, protection, and respect—this subject is discussed in more depth later in the book (see chapter 3). Some of the most difficult residents to deal with seemed to be suffering from one or more of those yearnings. Each resident was unique, each had a life story to tell, and each accomplished or went through things in their lives that they needed to share with others and did not want to be forgotten.

One resident was a constant complainer, and was not shy about letting his thoughts and feelings be known in a boisterous way. He was a World War II veteran and did not take kindly to a young man with long hair coming into his room. Every night as I delivered his dinner he would degrade me or yell obscenities at me. I did not take his attacks personally, because he didn't like anyone who came into his room, and he was this way with most employees. One evening as I was delivering his meal I was subjected to his usual ranting about how I had the freedom to have long hair because of his service in the war, and how I would never have gotten away with hair like that in his day.

But this day, instead of hurrying my duties so I could get in and out of his room before he could be mean to me, I asked him if I could come back after my shift so he could tell me his stories to help me understand what he went through, and why he disliked me. He agreed, and I kept my promise. When we met later that night he was more than eager to talk about his life and share his stories. I learned a great deal about him that evening, and this gave me a new respect for the man. I did not talk much; I just listened. This is the servant leader trait of listening. Not listening to hear, or listening to respond, but authentically listening because you care to hear what is said.

On my way home that night I wondered about the other residents. How many other amazing stories were left untold, how many other people had interesting stories to share, aching to be told? From that day forward I would enter each resident's room with a different perspective. And my attitude toward my job changed. It was no longer just a job; there was another dimension that made it enjoyable—it changed the meaning of a nursing home, into a nursing *home*, in the true sense of the word.

But it was not only the residents of the home I learned and grew from, there was also an amazing employee who worked there. Just like you might see in a movie, there was a wise old janitor who would listen to me complain about my life or other employees, and then offer me his priceless advice. Janitor Ray was short man with a stocky build who had a long black mustache and a beard like that of an Amish man. He was one of those types you could tell was well read and educated but did not feel the need to flaunt it. He did not talk a lot, but when he did, you knew something of importance was coming your way. Miraculously, he became my sage on the receiving dock.

Out of our many conversations, two things he said have stuck with me all of my years. First, when I would complain about the organization or management, he made the comment that what an organization lacks in substance, it will attempt to gain in glitter (or, in shop talk, "baffle them with BS"). An example of this was how management would stress cleaning and following procedures when the auditors were coming to recertify the organization, but then become lax in these duties, letting old ways resurface after the auditors left. Not only did these actions promote distrust in management, but they also created a lower standard of care and duty to the residents and for the organization itself.

Second, he taught me the story of the Chinese farmer. This story came up because, at the time, I was nineteen and living on my own. My girlfriend had moved in with me, both so we could be together and to help pay the rent. Being new to living life on my own presented many new challenges. Thankfully I found an empathetic and listening ear in Janitor Ray. One day on the receiving dock I told him my girlfriend was upset with me in the morning because I left toast crumbs in the butter container, and that the night before we were at a party and I was upset because I felt she was too friendly with her male friend who I did not know, but I would not admit I was jealous. Janitor Ray replied to me with the following story:

> One day a farmer noticed his prized horse had run away. The news spread throughout the village, and that evening his neighbors came over to say they were sorry for his bad luck. The farmer replied, "What is good, what is bad, we can never know." The next day the horse returned to the farm with six wild horses. This news spread, and later that evening his neighbors returned and congratulated the farmer on his good luck. The farmer replied, "What is good, what is bad, we can never know." The next day the farmer's son was attempting to break one of the wild horses and he was thrown off and broke his leg. This news spread, and later that evening the neighbors returned to say they were sorry for his bad luck. The farmer

replied, "What is good, what is bad, we can never know." Then the next day the army came knocking on every door in the village to recruit the young males to fight in a war. Since the son's leg was broken the army did not take him. This news spread, and later that evening the neighbors returned and congratulated the farmer on his good luck. The farmer once again replied, "What is good, what is bad, we can never know."

This story is a *life and leadership moment: What is good, what is bad?* Take the time needed to think through a situation or change before reacting. This philosophy has had a great impact on me. It has given me the ability to realize every bad thing can have a good side, and every good thing can have a bad side. It has also offered a valid reason to pause and examine decisions or events, and to think further about their effects or possible outcomes. But buyer beware, this philosophy also contains a hidden danger. One must be cognizant and not let this philosophy become too dominant in one's thought process. If taken too far, it could make one indifferent and apathetic to one's circumstances or toward the ones they love, and ruined relationships can result. What is good, what is bad; the wise use of this is an effective and valuable tool, but if taken too far . . . the story can fold in on itself.

I worked at the nursing home through most of my nineteenth year, and as I mentioned, I was enjoying the newfound freedom of my first apartment. It was the kind of apartment that during the day you were free to come and go, but at night it was wise to keep your travels short and few. After coming home from work and relaxing one evening, my phone rang and it was my father calling to say that a job was available where he worked, and it could be mine if I would only apply for it. He ended the conversation by saying this could be a job for life, and he stressed to me to make the right decision.

The next morning, I called in to my job at the nursing home and foolishly admitted to my supervisor that I would be late to work because I was going to interview for a different job. I was lucky to have landed the new job because when I arrived at work with my two-week notice in hand, she agreed it was good I got the job because otherwise I would have been fired on the spot.

I fulfilled my two weeks and went to work my first day carrying with me my work experience from the East Coast gas station and the Midwest nursing home, and these experiences provided the core foundation for how I would relate to people and eventually guide me into the position of leading others. Little did I know that these core experiences would create an internal conflict between what I felt to be my true nature and what the organization expected of me through leadership. This was truly the beginning of my leadership journey.

The manager who hired me was a tall, thin man a few years away from retirement. And by tall I mean that I'm six foot one inch myself, and I had to tilt my head up to look at to him. It was not his height that I respected, however, it was his leadership style. On my first day of employment, he told me that this was my job, to go learn it, and prove to him what I was capable of. This was a *life and leadership moment: you should train employees on what you want them to do and what needs to be done, then give them the freedom to learn and grow in their own way. Let them be in control of their own destiny and growth. Step in enough to coach, but step back enough to let go* (E. F. Johnson, personal communication, November 15, 2017).

For the first time in my work life I was free to try my own ideas and make my own mistakes. The manager let me have full control of my department and how it was laid out. Since this was my first experience with true autonomy on the job, I found it to be both exciting and challenging, and that in turn provided me with internal purpose and self-motivation. This was when I also discovered one of Murphy's Laws. It seemed whenever I sat down to take a break, my manager appeared on the floor to check on me. It always made me feel terrible because of the impression it gave, but it also taught me another *life and leadership moment: you cannot always trust your first impressions, snapshots of the moment, or a person's body language, mood, or tone of voice.*

A perfect example of how our experiences and preconceptions can affect our first impressions came to me in a sermon from Pastor Elias Kitoi Nasari, when he told the story of his first time coming to America. In his sermon he said that when his airplane was on its descent to land, he looked through the window and noticed that all the trees he saw had no leaves. At that moment he said he felt bad for America because he assumed that all of our trees had died. In Africa, the only trees that have no leaves are dead (personal communication, February 10, 2013). He had never seen or experienced a winter season as we in America know it, and he did not understand that deciduous trees lose their leaves in autumn. Although his story is on the extreme end, it shows that what we do not know can affect our perceptions and decision-making.

This story also sheds light into the subtle parts of our being and how our brain can trick us into assuming what we believe is truth. Daniel Gilbert, professor of psychology at Harvard University writes in his book *Stumbling on Happiness*, "The brain and the eye may have a contractual relationship in which the brain has agreed to believe what the eye sees, but in return the eye has agreed to look for what the brain wants" (2006, p. 183). Our brains perform this function automatically. We find convenient reasons for someone's actions or what their motivations may be, and then our biases help justify them with convenient and personalized reasons that we assume to be true. And we use these assumptions to defend, validate, or rationalize the situation to ourselves with no substantial evidence or facts.

For example, an employee came into work one day who was not acting like himself. In our conversations, his answers were unusually short and lacked his common friendliness. I assumed the employee's negative demeanor was because the previous day I had reinstated for him an unfavorable job function. My brain agreed to believe what I was seeing, and my eyes led me to believe what it was looking for—a quick and easy answer to the situation, regardless of what might be the real reason for the employee's actions. I simply assumed he was still upset with me for reinstating the task or for something else I did, and I proceeded to avoid him for much of the morning to allow him time to cool off from a situation that I imagined I was responsible for.

After the morning passed, there was no change in the employee's demeanor. I decided to approach him to ask if everything was okay, to dig a little deeper and find out if I was truly the cause of his unhappiness. The employee then told me that his mother was hurt in a car accident the night before, and he was worried and thinking about her. Up until then I had convinced myself I was the cause of the situation, but by being authentically curious, asking questions, and listening, the true context of the situation was revealed.

I believe these two short examples provide reason enough for leaders not to assume what they see or feel from their first impressions but to instead become active and authentic listeners, and use the power of open communication to help discover the truth; both of which are powerful tools used by the servant leader. An additional example that describes the process also works as a tip for public speaking. This is something I learned from another pastor, Pastor Sue, whose sermons I always anticipated and enjoyed when she preached. I was specifically interested in how she wrote her amazing sermons that kept worshippers on the edge of their seats.

A little background: well into the future, when I was forty-six years old, I had completed my undergraduate degree and was considering pursuing a master's degree in theology. It was around then that I met with Pastor Sue, and I had arranged a meeting with her to discuss her preaching talent and learn more about life in ministry. Before we discussed her preaching style, she asked me some specific questions about why I was considering going into the ministry. As I heard myself respond, I knew that if I decided to pursue this career I would have much soul-searching to do. After that she graciously offered her technique for crafting her amazing sermons. She said she would take a piece of paper and draw a line down the middle. On the top left she wrote "Content," and on the top right she wrote "Context," and then she notated her bullet points down the paper on each side.

Life and leadership moment: you can use this technique to improve your leadership today. When you encounter a situation, first realize that your thoughts may not be your own or a true representation of the situation. Create a page in your mind. List the content of the situation on the left side, and possible context (reasons for) on the right. Then, instead of assuming what you originally think and feel is the truth, approach the situation openly and ask questions with the purpose of understanding and uncovering the truth to discover the actual situation or problem.

Back to the example of sitting down and taking a break: maybe my manager at this time had the experience to know this, or he had his own personal reasons to not to judge snapshots so quickly, because he never once questioned me or made me feel bad when he found me sitting down on the job.

Therefore, I believe, leaders should never assume the worst upon first sight or rely on the hearsay of another before learning all they can about a situation; however, managers must react when they become aware of conflicting information. It is the duty of a new and emerging leader to verify or debunk the information by using the servant leader quality of authentic listening. Unfortunately, this is never an easy or desirable task. As someone who has been in this situation, I discovered that there is a fine line between discovering the truth and the possibility of creating feelings of distrust for management and in the processes and relationships in the hierarchy of the organization.

If you have a manager who jumps the gun and accuses an employee of a new and emerging leader of this based on hearsay, there is no good way to approach the situation other than from the heart. This is easier said than done because it usually involves questioning the motives and actions of your top reports. So stay calm and discover if there is any validity to the accusations. If there is, admit it, and look for a way to improve it. But if it is unwarranted, figure out the content and the context and reply with the facts. I know this, too, is easier said than done when this sort of questioning and distrust comes your way. When it is truly unwarranted it feels like a personal attack on you or your team, and it is one of the most demotivating and trust-killing ways a manager can negatively affect their core crew. But that is most likely insecurity and bad leadership on their part, not yours.

I was very grateful then to have such an aware and understanding manager. I found him to be a great leader and motivator, but my immediate supervisor was the darkness to his light. This supervisor had a leadership style that was the opposite of anything I had experienced before, and by opposite, I mean nonexistent. Yes, he ensured that what needed to be manufactured, tested, and shipped was in the queue to be completed, but how and when this happened was left solely to the competence of the employees. There was no coaching, and discipline was only executed by elevated interference from the supervisor's boss or human resources department.

Whenever the supervisor was approached with a personnel problem, his most common response was "I hear ya." Sure, he would hear what was making his reports in the department unhappy, but that was as far as he would go toward creating solutions. I bring this up because the lack of supervision affected employee morale and how fast and well product was produced. This supervisor was in charge of a distribution department, and as anyone in charge of one can attest, the department gets hit from both ends every day: receiving is busy in the morning and shipping is busy at the end of the day. I divert to this now because this is where another *life and leadership moment surfaces: when you get good in, you have a higher chance of getting good out.*

This concept applies to people as well as product. For product, the faster you can supply production with the parts and quantities they need, the faster production can produce product and the faster shipping can ship. The more accurate and repeatable these processes, the more accurate the promises to the customer are. So my supervisor's lack of listening skills and leadership not only jeopardized on-time delivery, but it also meant that I would be on my own in a frenzied rush at the end of the day to get all the orders packed and processed before the package carriers arrived for pickup.

To help make my work life easier I began to teach myself skills outside of my current job description involving how to build, test, and schedule product to be made. I would perform these jobs when others were absent and help other employees who were behind when I sensed customer orders were at risk of not shipping. I performed these tasks well enough to take over when my supervisor was absent or on vacation. But what was unusual was when the supervisor was not at work is when he did his best supervising. When the supervisor was absent, he would repeatedly call me throughout the day to dictate what he thought I should be doing, and how and when to do it. It was not long before I stopped answering the phone and instead performed the job in my own way.

His lack of structure, discipline, integrity, and his unpredictability caused excessive and unnecessary amounts of stress for employees in the shop and office. This type of leadership led only to frustration and decreased morale, and I found myself performing damage control for the shop and office employees as a result of his actions.

Director and endowed professor of the D. B. Reinhart Institute for Ethics Richard Kyte once said something simple but important in class when discussing life and leadership: *life and leadership moment: "a bad manager equals a bad life."* If you have a good day at work you will leave the building feeling accomplished, happy, and looking forward to life outside of the organization. If you have a bad day at work because of a bad manager it makes your day that much more intolerable, and when you leave the organization that day you never really leave. Your negative thoughts and emotions travel with you. Have you ever had a bad day at work and on the way home you drive faster and more aggressively, have you ever become more intolerant of people in public or unjustly mean to the ones you love over something that usually would not be an issue? A bad manager can produce a negative ripple effect into the community.

Kyte also enlightened me with another wise thought that day, which is another *life and leadership moment: "anyone can lead, they can always serve as a bad example."* Using my leader as an example, I vowed that if I ever got the chance to step up to the supervisor position, I would try never to repeat his ways and strive to do better for those I was responsible to and for. The compassion and empathy that was lacking in the leadership I was under enhanced my desire to be true to myself and others. As I would later find out, compassion and empathy are also traits of a servant leader; if only I could find a way to merge my inner perceptions of leadership with the outer expectations of the organization for a supervisor.

CHAPTER 2

Primary Growth

This second stage focuses on growth and development.

"When we change our question from what we want to what is being asked of us, our conscious is opened up and we allow ourselves to be influenced by it" (Greenleaf 2002, p. 7).

This stressful scenario at work would continue for eight years, but during this period there were significant changes affecting the nation's workplaces, one of which is especially worthy of mention. It touches on the servant leader traits of empathy, awareness, and commitment to the growth of people.

Emma Dill wrote in her 2018 article that "Jenson v. Eveleth Tachonite Co. became the first sexual-harassment class action suit tried in U.S. federal court," beginning circa 1987 and concluding in 1998. This introduced major changes at my organization, as it did for organizations across the country. Pin-up girl calendars were popular and hanging up at almost every workstation in my workplace, but after the court's decision upper management came out to the shop and demanded that all the calendars be removed. They also made my supervisor remove a large box of pornographic magazines that he had been collecting and hiding in the back of the shop.

Not long after that, the Human Resources Department began having company meetings and requiring training on how to identify and prevent sexual harassment. Of all the sexual harassment prevention training I have participated in over my lifetime, I believe the most powerful and significant prevention-training "video" was actually watching the film *North Country* (released in 2005), which is about the *Jenson v. Eveleth Tachonite Company* class-action lawsuit. It is my belief that this movie should be required viewing for every employee. If you watch the movie, you may acquire a greater understanding of the issue of sexual harassment and how it can affect people on and off the job. Training is of course essential, but when the issue really "hits home"—as it did for me when I saw *North Country*—that's when people internalize it.

Near the end of the eight years of stress, my original manager retired and a new one was hired. The new manager was heavily focused on results and efficiency. In a short time, he was able to assess the climate and state of the shop, and it was not long before my supervisor was terminated and an opening to fill that position was posted. There were two employees who applied for the supervisor position: another shop employee and I. We both were capable of doing the job.

The other employee was a short man who had an even shorter fuse. One story of many I could share about his temper was on one hot summer day (summers at work were brutal; the building did not have air conditioning and the building had a low tin roof), I was watching him form a metal ring by tapping it with a hammer around a cylinder. As he hammered in the heat, his glasses slid down his sweaty nose. He pushed them back up and continued hammering. They slid down again, he pushed them up again. They slid down a third time, but instead of pushing them up, he threw his glasses down on his workbench and used his hammer to smash them into oblivion while shouting loud obscenities with each hammer strike.

Although this man's outbursts provided many needed moments of comic relief, I believe they were one of the main reasons I was chosen over him for the supervisor position. When it was announced I got the job, the other man quit the organization the next day. In retrospect, this was likely to be in my favor because I didn't think ahead about how I would have dealt with a disgruntled employee with a short fuse who now felt slighted. The best part of that promotion was that for about six months I was my father's supervisor before he retired.

Since I was promoted, I decided to cut my waist-long hair to better fit the supervisory role. The woman who cut my hair also worked at the organization, but unbeknownst to me she was in cahoots with my father. When she cut my hair she saved my long ponytail, and gave it to my father the next morning before I arrived. When I got in to work, I walked past my father sitting at his workbench, and there was my ponytail attached to the back of his head via a baseball cap. Although my father did this to poke fun at me, I found myself overwhelmed by a strong sense of empathy. When I saw my ponytail hanging from my father's head, I suddenly understood what he may have seen when he looked at me. At that moment I truly realized the love he showed me by accepting me for who I was.

Empathy played a much stronger role in my life going forward that day. It was obvious to me that my title over my father was in name only, but I was proud to have him be a witness to my growth in the company. After my father retired, and time progressed, I realized no one had replaced me as lead of the department. I was doing more lead duties and working instead of being a supervisor. I knew there was a better way to be a leader to the employees and a better way to treat them compared to what had been the norm during recent years. Something inside me wanted to help do that, but I also realized through honest self-awareness and reflection, both servant leader traits, that I was just not ready or prepared for a supervisory role at that point. I began to realize that what I wanted to do, and what was being asked of me, presented internal contradictions for me.

John Heider, author of *The Tao of Leadership*, wrote that "enlightened leadership is service, not selfishness. The leader grows more and lasts longer by placing the well-being of all above the well-being of self." *Life and leadership moment: be honest with yourself and your intuitions, even though it may require the delay of self-gratification and fulfillment. Will the decisions you make today be made for yourself, or the people you serve?* This decision was the beginning of my entry into the servant leader trait of stewardship; that is, the looking after, being responsible for, and making the best decisions for what and/or whom one is in charge or in control of. My conscious was beginning to open up, and I just needed to find the right influence and direction to match where my internal compass was pointing me.

Not long after my promotion, the organization acquired its first company. Because I had been hesitant to take on the supervisory role, management filled the position with the acquired company's supervisor, and I got the title of assistant supervisor. I was thankful that the organization still believed in me, and they soon enrolled me in a supervisory-training class at the local chamber of commerce. The training consisted of six modules that were led by a very charismatic instructor who used a student-centered learning approach. This kind of instructor and style of teaching helped spark my interest in the course. Hindsight reveals an important *life and leadership moment: most people who do not continue education after high school view their graduation as the end point of their continued learning. If we, as servant leaders, want to interest others to learn and grow, we must acknowledge this and strive to change their perception of learning. We have to make learning applicable, interesting, and personal to their life experiences.*

I enjoyed the supervisory classes, but it is unfortunate that I did not retain the six binders of information. If I had, I could better reflect and compare that information to what I have learned over the years, or maybe what I just did not understand at that time. What I do recall is that the courses provided many applicable and interesting aspects of leadership, and my class-mates' discussions and their interpretations and struggles with leadership were interesting. My memory of the curriculum and discussions recalls many black-and-white solutions that pro-vided me with little to no application in our full-colored world, and this was something I would struggle with for the majority of my leadership journey.

The solutions to workplace issues offered in these classes only worked well if there were little to no concern for people's emotions, work conditions, or underlying issues that may have led up to those situations. It gave me the impression that policy and office politics trumped worker issues and dissensions—and dissent is important. Jane Jacobs, an American Canadian jour-nalist, author, theorist, and activist wrote, "Consider that every single improvement in efficiency of production or distribution requires dissent from the way things were previously done" (1992, p. 41). The caveat to this is that organizational change never happens overnight, whether it be a public or private orga-nization. The message here is persistence and dedication to change, but change is one of the hardest things to implement and for people to accept. Which brings us to the next *life and leadership moment: leaders and people tend to react to situations and circumstances like water and electricity; both may gravitate toward the path of least resistance and not realize it.*

If you have ever noticed a building or park where there is a sidewalk or walkway, but people have instead created their own paths or shortcuts through the grass resulting in dirt paths, this is what I'm talking about. In a case like this it's bad design, and when employees use the path of least resistance to undermine the job or the organization, it may be a reflection of bad leadership. When leaders use the path of least resistance, combined with power, control, and self-serving interests, we only need to use our imagination or watch the evening news to be reminded of the consequences.

But the path of least resistance can also be of benefit. I noticed one day that some wire racks in my warehouse were being returned to the bays on angles instead of straight back inside of the racking areas, and the racks would protrude out into the aisles. This practice gave an unruly impression and created a safety issue for fork-truck operation in the warehouse. By using the theory of the path of least resistance to examine how people were using the warehouse, I was able to adjust the number and orientation of the racks to eliminate the hazard and make the jobs of inventory control and material handlers more efficient. There are always two sides to every coin; try to find the positive side and use that to your advantage.

The short leadership class I took did give me a base to call home where there wasn't one before, but I would remain in a sort of leadership stasis for many years. I could understand the black-and-white parts, but I would often struggle with the gray areas and what I felt was right to me—how to incorporate myself into my leadership style and still satisfy management's wants. So I instead relied on focusing on treating people right and as fairly as I could. Along the way, I would pick up tidbits of sayings or teachings that justified my internal cause. A couple examples that I found were (1) not ask anyone to do something I would not do myself, and (2) not let my mistakes become someone else's headaches. I also learned that sometimes you may have to break these rules, and if I did I would always offer my help, admit my shortcomings, and apologize for the mistakes I made, which helped to relieve frustrations and improve relationships. This reflects the servant leader trait of building community and increasing trust.

At this point in my story, I could go on and on about the employees I have encountered and the many crazy stories associated with them. A word of caution. As you become a better leader and listener, be aware that people may tell you things you are not expecting to hear. Being a leader opens you up to people's lives and sometimes these things are disturbing. I could also discuss and reflect on the different and opposing types of leadership that have come and gone, all with equally interesting and alarming content, but that would be material for a different type of book. My aim is to keep the chapters short to get to the fundamentals of servant leadership. So hold tight, we are almost there.

Fast-forward many years and the organization became good at acquiring other companies. When I found myself on the opposite side of that equation, and my organization was acquired, it scared the hell out of me and made me question and doubt my future with the organization. I found out that a coworker had gone back to school for an undergraduate degree in business. I thought to myself that that would be good for me because if I were terminated I would have a better chance to rebound at another job. Not long after that realization, at the green and growing age of forty-one, I, too, became a college student.

One night while attending my third class, and after the student introductions, someone in my cohort said I was old enough to be the father of all my classmates. That moment of brief embarrassment helped elevate my perception of continued education from a career cushion or ladder-climbing tool to something that would improve understanding of myself and the world around me. After four introductory classes, my fifth class was Introduction to Business Ethics, where I wrote my first paper on leadership titled "Ethics and the Role of Leadership." Reading this after some years I can see that I had two main thoughts in this short paper: (1) the importance of both the leader and followers, and (2) the difference between managing and leading. Below are the last four paragraphs from that paper. In hindsight, it shows me that I was already on a path to servant leadership, but I was unaware of its existence at the time.

> Managing is different than leading. Managing is concerned with the questions of how decisions are made, and leading is concerned with what decisions are made. Leaders must make all stakeholders aware of the fact that all involved in the business contribute to the success of the business. Leaders must participate in the organization, trust the subordinates, and let others take risks to enhance their creativity and innovation.

I have learned that being a leader is not just giving people what they want or telling them what they like to hear; this is servicing not leading. Just like it takes three logs to start a fire; leaders, followers, and goals are the three parts that combine to support leadership. Every level of management must commit to ethical behavior; one incident of mistrust or loss of confidence ripples through an organization like a sound wave that can affect everyone in the organization. Being an interactive leader is not a weakness. This style can enhance people's self-worth by encouraging participation, sharing power and information, creating loyalty through trust and respect, and promoting the flow of information. Along with good pay, people want to know they are contributing to a higher purpose and have an opportunity to learn and grow.

I look toward my superiors to conduct business with integrity and fairness by doing the right things, treating people right, and producing results that are just to all (and I will no longer belittle myself to refer to those as my superiors, they will now be referred to as the people I report to). I also realize that others are looking for me to act in the same respect.

The biggest challenge facing me will be upholding my principals of inner morals and

ethics; instead of taking the easy way out or following the paths of others around me. I believe the
combination of my moral compass and reasoned
analysis will provide me with the right tools to
make the right decisions. (Osborne 2013, p. 3)

These are some truly bold statements, and as you can
imagine, this time of my life was a major turning point in my
self-perception, my perception of the work world around me, and
what my conscious was saying that leadership could be. About
a year later I was enrolled in another Business Ethics class. But
this time my cohort was broken up, and this particular class was
the first one where every student was a stranger to the other. The
professor of this class was unlike any I had had before.

He started the first class by using introductions like
every other instructor, but something was different this time.
He somehow crafted his questions and responses in a way that
brought this class of strangers closer together, and by the start
of the second class the next week all the students realized they
had at least one thing in common with each other. I also realized
that some previous biases I had toward others in the class had
been eliminated. And somehow, in this short amount of time,
this professor had quickly and successfully created a small community in that classroom.

I discovered that I knew people in common with a couple of my classmates, and others discovered they had worked at
similar places. The sense of community that was created in the

classroom helped improve learning and also increased participation in the dreaded team projects. I was intrigued by what I experienced and the abundance of community that was created before my eyes in that classroom, so I stayed after class that second night to ask the professor what he did to accomplish this. I knew that whatever he did, and however he did it, it was something I needed to learn and apply in my life.

When I asked the professor what his secret was, he told me he was using the philosophy of servant leadership. He then gave me a brief overview of Robert Greenleaf's theory as well as the authors of a few books he said I should read. His teaching style combined with his ability to create community was the catalyst that set me on the path to servant leadership. The remaining years of my undergraduate experience were now focused on seeking servant leadership knowledge from any source I could talk to, read, or be taught by.

Not long after this class I found out about the Servant Leader Cities Tours and would attend the conferences whenever they came to town. This in turn led to my awareness of the master's degree in servant leadership offered at Viterbo University in La Crosse, Wisconsin, where I graduated from in 2021, and here we are having this conversation today. What I would learn at Viterbo would provide the answers to the questions, uncertainties, reservations, and doubts I had about leadership, and solidify the purpose and structure for my leadership in an ever-changing and uncertain world. This led to the next stage of my leadership journey.

CHAPTER 3

Secondary Growth

**When the roots begin to spread, they provide
the tree with a more secure foundation.**

*"If you enter an organization with the intent of helping . . . person
and team . . . if you enter it with the hope that your intervention
will help the relationship to better serve all concerned, then I urge
you to consider . . . the impediments you will surely find. . . . Will
you regard these impediments as error . . . to change or correct, or
will you regard them as illness in which your relationship is that of
healing agent" (Greenleaf 1996, p. 92)?*

What I observed attending the Servant Leader Cities Tours was
that the attendees seemed to ask the same questions at every
conference; that is, how do you improve an organization that
views its employees as resources instead of sources, how do you
change an organization's culture to a servant leader culture, how
can I apply this theory in my organization, or, in short, how do
you go about doing it? Like many things in life the answers are
easy, but the application is where things get complicated.

If you are a new and emerging leader and contemplating introducing servant leadership to your organization, or if you're just trying to make your home or work life better, this chapter will offer some of what I have learned and observed over the years in an attempt to assist you on your journey. The first step is to be clear and honest with yourself. You need to determine your level of passion for, and how dedicated, committed, or loyal you are to the organization and/or the people associated with it. Being clear, honest, and direct with yourself at this stage can save you from much unneeded stress, strife, conflict, and many sleepless nights.

The good news is that this decision to introduce servant leadership in or for your organization may be the easiest one to make. The decision will be based on the new and emerging leader's commitment, passion, and relationship with the organization and level of community that exists within. Whether you envision your employment as temporary or long term, the servant leader goal is the same: to improve the way you treat others and commit yourself to making the organization, individuals, and community better in whatever way you can. After you have contemplated these points and decide to move forward, you will need to understand your organization.

Author Barry Schwartz said something interesting about many of today's organizations: that "previously a company might define itself as a manufacturer of cloth that endeavored to make cloth manufacturing profitable, [but] now that company would define itself as a pursuer of profit that happens to manufacture cloth" (2000, p. 46). The difference between these two perceptions is immense; one can almost feel the difference. How much do you believe this statement relates to your organization? It is one of many ways to judge a bit more deeply the health and purpose of an organization. For instance, are the mission and vision statements of the organization actually talked about, observed, and "felt" in the way it operates and the conversations that are had? Reflecting on this will help to determine the path you may choose to walk.

Understanding the Organization

Assessment

Attempting to change something as important as culture and leadership style is very risky, especially if those in power do not know or understand much about what servant leadership is. If servant leadership is new or a foreign concept, I like to use the analogy of rolling a snowball up a mountain for initiating the change. We can assume that the climate on a mountain will change from the base up to the summit, and implementing servant leadership can be like rolling a snowball up that mountainside. If you start from the bottom and try to roll it uphill, the bigger it gets, and the colder it gets, the more difficult it is to move. You may even feel your feet slip out from under you as you push.

What way do you think your snowball will be rolling as you introduce this concept to the organization's "mountain"? Will it be like rolling the servant leadership snowball up- or downhill, or will it be more like circling up the mountain in a slow ascent? What is the current style of leadership? Are the CEO and leadership team dedicated to leadership? If not, what is their purpose and who or what is dictating it? What will be your elevator pitch to introduce what you believe and feel about servant leadership, and is there anyone you think may be more receptive to the philosophy?

What about the other levels of management or those you report to and those who report to you? Who in the organization might oppose you or be tough to convince? What may be their reasons for opposing you personally or servant leadership in general? What other obstacles or challenges might hinder your progress? Are there biases? Is there apathy or indifference in the organization? Do silos exist between departments? Are there any types of prejudices, either obvious or flying beneath the radar? Is there a lack of trust, arrogance, or fear in the organization? Are there any obstacles in terms of processes and procedures?

Is the Human Resources Department involved in the day-to-day operations? Who there might you need to begin a relationship with? Is there a leadership-training program in place, and if so, how well does it complement the qualities of a servant leadership mindset? Have you considered talking to other people or departments, from maintenance to sales to marketing to engineering? If you found someone and they got on board with you, what skills, abilities or leverage do they have that may be used in a positive way?

Answering these questions is not an easy or quick thing to do, but neither is changing the climate or culture of an organization. I hope you can understand by the scope of these questions that you cannot, and should not, take on this responsibility by yourself. You will need to begin to build a community around you; building this community is the only way you can develop a servant leader atmosphere, and it all starts with that first person you inspire to join your quest.

Social Capital and Trust

Photo 112127706 © Bennnn | Dreamstime.com

Whether you are building a servant leadership community, a grass-roots movement, or an impromptu dance party, you need to get that first follower to make others feel safer to join the movement. We've all known that person with the personality that lights up a room, the personality that makes people gravitate toward and want to be around them. If you can find someone like this to be your first follower, or if you can create that type of feeling yourself, you may have won the servant leadership lottery. But the odds of winning this lottery are slim, and waiting to hit it will only delay your cause.

You can instead start to create and increase social capital among your team and coworkers. Social capital refers to the relationships, on both the horizontal and vertical planes, that allow an organization to be effective and efficient. It is important to understand that there are two types of social capital. Robert Putnam, who is the author of *Bowling Alone* (a book about social capital in America) says, "Bonding social capital constitutes a kind of sociological superglue, whereas bridging social capital provides a sociological WD-40" (2000, p. 250). Like the mortar between bricks, bonding capital does just what its name suggests: it creates a tighter and healthier bond between people, and the force that helps the bonding capital molecules stick is called trust.

Trust is important to the creation of any community, but Putnam contends that there are competing forces that prohibit the workplace from enhancing public and personal life, such as the fact that employees do not join together in after-work and outside-the-job activities or organizations. Further, a community at work does not help those who are unemployed. Considering that many established social organizations of the past are seeing declines in membership, I believe the opposite of Putnam's viewpoint can be true—that the workplace may be one of the last places for establishing a community inside and outside of the organization. Establishing a community of trust in the workplace is the first step to creating a community outside of it.

It has been said that employees today spend more time at work than with their families, and, the Coronavirus pandemic notwithstanding, where else today will a group of people come together for that amount of time? And why would we not want to make the workplace a place where good comes in and good goes out? As Richard Kyte said in class once, "When you see good community you want to be part of it." A good community attracts people in the same way the person with the magnetic personality attracts others.

Trust creates an unspoken bond in the organization, it creates a bond with its culture and leadership, and trust enables and empowers its employees to feel free to unleash their inner talents. But don't just take my opinions about trust as a given, here are some of the things researchers and experts have to say. A study appearing in *Economics and Sociology* states that "from an organizational perspective, trust is critical for minimizing uncertainty, risks and operating costs, enhancing employees' commitment and productivity . . . learning . . . knowledge sharing . . . organizational innovativeness and innovation. . . . An organization that operates in a low-trust framework will effectively see the opposite attributes develop in the attitudes and behavior of its employees" (Pucetaite, Novelskaite, and Markunaite 2015, p. 11).

Harvard professor and former CEO of Semco Inc, Ricardo Semler wrote that a

> naturally evolving and shared culture bonds people within a company, and it's founded on trust. You cannot have integrity, dissent, respect, or open communication without it. . . . That only works if people trust each other and trust the company. . . . If they know there are falsehoods or deceptions, their willingness to associate with the company diminishes. Soon they'll be working there just for the paycheck, and be embarrassed to tell anyone. (2004, p. 122)

Employees monitor their leaders' actions and organizational environment to determine whether to trust management, and that determination will dictate how the employees respond (McCauley and Kuhnert 1992). Employees will also associate their supervisors' or managers' trustworthiness with top management. I know from my personal experience that I would observe how my leaders acted and reacted on a daily basis as a way to judge my responses. Leadership and business best-selling authors Kouzes and Posner discuss the importance of a leader's trustworthiness. They wrote that one question can make the greatest difference in an employee's motivation and performance: "Is this person worthy of my trust? If the answer is yes, follow. If your answer is I don't know, get more information, and get it fast. But, if your answer is no, find another job or . . . another leader. . . .

Every time you follow someone you do not trust you erode your self-esteem. . . . Your worth depreciates, and you become less valuable to yourself and others" (2011, p. 18).

Life and leadership moment: trust in an organization is like the purpose of a downtown's one-way and two-way streets: they both exist together to move people in an efficient and effective way that makes full use of the community. Using the street analogy, let us take a brief ride through the downtown streets of trust to understand how trust in an organization is developed. There are four streets of trust that determine the type, amount, and quality of trust in and between an organization's employees.

The first set of streets are one-way streets, and their names are Cognitive and Affective. These streets direct the traffic of two types of trust that originate from inside an employee and are produced by one's internal beliefs and biases. As we drive down Cognitive Street, we find this type of trust allows the rationality of what a person experiences, believes, and senses to arrive at this first trust destination. For example, positive trust experiences the employee has had with a leader will lead the employee to believe that the leader is trustworthy. The employee will then have a strong sense going forward that the leader will continue this behavior when additional trust issues arise.

As we drive down Affective Street, we find it is an extension of Cognitive Street. Affective trust develops from an employee's emotions to produce positive feelings of confidence and an enhanced level of care and concern for the leader. In conclusion, these one-way streets run parallel to each other and work together by combining the employee's experiences, what the employee expects to experience, and what the employee's collective knowledge and perceptions are that add up to create their level of trust in a leader and organization.

The second set of streets are two-way streets. The first street is called Lateral Street and it runs east and west. Lateral trust comes from the relationships between employees that have similar jobs, responsibilities, or authority in an organization. For example, do all the frontline workers trust each other, and do they trust the other departments' workers they have contact with? These people are often the largest groups in an organization, and developing and maintaining trust among them is a difficult and ongoing task, but one that is essential. Keeping trust amongst these employees helps ensure higher levels of happiness, comradery, security, and the degree of community the employees feel.

The second of the two-way streets is called Vertical Street, and this street runs north and south. Vertical trust comes from the relationship between the levels of authority or hierarchy in an organization. Do the employees trust their low-level management, the low-level their mid-level, the mid-level their the mid-management, and so on (or any combination thereof), and do those levels of trust work or feel the same in the reverse? *Life and leadership moment: your position as a new and emerging servant leader means you are often the mediator between the employee-management road. As you stand in the middle of this proverbial two-way street there is a sense of danger because you risk getting hit from both directions.*

We must understand that we have responsibilities to both our reports and our managers. Former president and CEO of the Robert Greenleaf Center for Servant Leadership Larry Spears says, "Remember, the word responsible means *able to respond*" (1998, p. 25). Sometimes the hardest part is learning how to properly respond to satisfy the needs of your reports and the wants of your managers. It is a very peculiar situation. For your reports, you are their leader, and have the responsibility to provide them with what they legitimately *need*. For your managers, you are their service provider, and your responsibility is to give them what they *want*, when they want it.

Let's look at this more closely. As you grow in your role, and increase your understanding of how your business operates, you may find yourself torn between these two worlds, encountering the paradox of not being able to provide the *needs* because the *wants* override what you believe would make things better for your reports. *Life and leadership moment: always remember who you are working for, and do not let the reports' needs override and dictate what you believe the wants are, you need to give management what they want first, as hard and difficult as this may be. After you give management what they want, then you can concentrate on the needs of your reports.* Ultimately, it is up to you to decide what battles you want to fight, and which hill you could or should die on. Just remember, "He who fights and runs away may live to fight another day; but he who is battle slain can never rise to fight again" (Goodreads 2021).

Amidst this struggle, your job is to recognize your ability to determine which streets of trust have road construction that are slowing down or stopping community traffic and figure out a way to improve that flow as soon as possible in any way you can. A good word to describe a new and emerging servant leader is "conduit." The Latin root of "conduit" is "conductus," which means "to bring together." As a servant leader your job is to bring together the two opposing perspectives and perceptions between employees and management, and to stand in the middle of the street to create harmony, community, and keep the traffic flowing. Remember Greenleaf's words at the start of this chapter: if you approach this paradox from a healing perspective rather than a controlling and correcting one, it can help alleviate some stress during these situations.

Communication

Life and leadership moment: I have discovered that most grievances in an organization occur when employees feel useless, powerless, and faceless. Kyte commented in a class lecture on March 23, 2018, that "once people lose community they fill it with other things, and then it's harder to get it back; people forget that they need community to be happy." There is power and safety in numbers. Political commentator and author Thomas Friedman said that "when people feel embedded in a community, they feel protected, respected, and connected . . . it generates enormous trust" (2016, p. 359), and when there is trust, people are much more apt to feel like they can communicate openly.

I like to rearrange Friedman's words to read connected, protected, and respected to help us remember his quote, and I will refer to them as CPR #1 going forward. Through my experience I have learned that most employees' complaints, criticisms, anger, and personnel issues typically stem from one, or a combination of these three concepts. For example, not feeling connected comes from being left out of decision-making, or the employee not feeling like they are part of the team or group. Not feeling protected or safe in the workplace: the leader does not correct issues caused by other employees or departments. And not respected: the opinions, feelings, needs of the employee or job are ignored and pleas for change are unheard and not acted on. And sometimes the issues are not revealed upfront, and it will take listening, empathy, and patience to uncover the real reason(s) before it comes to the surface. The purpose of CPR #1, like the original acronym of CPR (cardiopulmonary resuscitation), is to restore the function of circulation and breathing. In a leadership sense it serves as a baseline to help renew an employee's trust in their leaders and organization, and help leaders to correct wrongs and right issues.

While CPR #1 is the underlying reason issues arise most of the time, sometimes the issues stem from the leader. The way the leader acts and treats others can have a major effect on morale and motivation. This is where CPR #2 comes into play, and I would like to introduce three more characteristics of the servant leader to the list. If the leader does not act in a consistent, persistent, and resilient way, issues often appear, sooner or later. For instance, do we act in a consistent and fair manner to all people all of the time? How persistent are we in our actions, both in good times and times of difficulty? How resilient are we when we react to opposition or difficulty? Can we withstand and recover quickly from adversity and remain optimistic?

As a new and emerging leader, it is important to remember that it takes time to build trust, and that all that hard work can be lost in an instant. Therefore, having an environment where authentic communication is practiced, biases are exposed and eliminated, and an atmosphere where employees are free to speak their truths creates the trust needed to achieve real teamwork. As mentioned earlier, employees are always watching their leaders and the organization for clues to help them decide who and how much they will trust. If leaders do not act in a consistent, persistent, and resilient way, people will notice, and then the grapevine will do the rest of the work. Being cognizant and practicing CPR #2 will go a long way toward creating a stable environment. The policies, rules, and changes to daily routines of the organization also play a part. This can be amplified if the employees do not have a say in decisions, are afraid to offer dissent, do not feel listened to, or cannot have a tough discussion in a civilized manner. Behaving in a consistent, persistent, and resilient way are essential to creating trust, which is essential to keeping the lines of communication open.

Often it is the lack of communication that creates a gap between what employees feel and what they are told. The more truth you can give about the reasons behind a decision may not make employees feel better, but it may help them understand the processes by which decisions were made. *Life and leadership moment: Being a lead or supervisor often means that one must put a good face on unfavorable news, changes, or decisions by upper management. I like to repeat what Edward Johnson, my undergraduate teacher for a class on human resource management, said, "This is called being able to take shit and sell it as ice cream." Relaying unfavorable news is just part of the job. But be mindful, if you find yourself selling more ice cream than leading, then someone else may be a better salesperson than you at selling that cold, refreshing treat.*

You'll also want to keep in mind that being an effective ice-cream salesperson often relies on knowing the buzzwords, catchphrases, and slogans the organization uses to enhance its purpose and pursue its goals. These are important to know not only if you're presenting difficult news but also if you want to make change, as using them in your proposals will help you gain attention and interest. So find out what they are and insert them into your everyday vocabulary because this type of communication will get more attention and concern for the issues you want to correct or change.

Another of my undergraduate teachers, Marjorie Lang, made a comment in class one evening that has always stuck with me. She said that "you buy hot dogs from vendors, you buy parts from suppliers." For me, this defined a shift in my perception of business relationships. A vendor is an entity one obtains a product or service from that one does not need a relationship or contract with. A supplier is an entity where the organization depends on both a contract and/or relationship to provide the best price, quality, and service for an organization's needs.

Many people in my organization would use the words "vendor" and "supplier" interchangeably when referring to its suppliers. I once decided to begin a quiet campaign to change the words and the mindset of the organization when referring to its suppliers. For example, during conversation or in emails, when employees would use the term "vendor," I would reply using "supplier," and if an employee continued using the wrong term, I would use the hot dog example to illustrate my intentions. By my being persistent and using persuasion, employees did begin to use the word "supplier" instead of "vendor" in conversations. (But bear in mind that as employees come and go, changing the language culture could be an everlasting task.)

One final thought about word choice. *Life and leadership moment: make sure you understand the true meaning of words before you use them. Words may often sound similar but have different meanings and implications. Ensure the words you use imply and convey the message you intend to communicate, so that you are not dissuading employees or pushing an unintended agenda or goal.* I bring this up because it is important to be aware of the content and context of what is being said.

I once heard a trainer in an Occupational and Safety and Health Administration training course say that the solution to pollution is dilution. I disagree with this statement because the contaminate does not actually go away, and will eventually resurface at a later date. Leaders need to be aware of conversations that may dilute or pollute the engagement or motivation of employees in an organization. Know that I'm not implying that you should scrutinize every single word heard or said, but just be aware of what you, the organization, or other managers are conveying: do not take everything you hear with a grain of salt, but make sure what *you* say originates from your heart, your soul, and a dictionary.

I mention this because I have witnessed the effects of inaccurate terminology on the people they were spoken to. An example of this is that a leader may use the words "dedicate," "commit," and "loyal" in an interchangeable way in meetings or conversations. On the surface these words may seem to have similar meanings, but their true meanings indicate otherwise. "Dedicate" refers to devoting time and effort to a task or purpose, "commit" refers to being dedicated to a cause or activity, and "loyal" refers to firm and constant allegiance to a person or institution.

For example, I may dedicate my time to finish writing this book, I may commit myself to volunteering at the local community meal program, or I may be loyal to my spouse or profession by taking an oath, affirmation, or pledge of office before assuming the responsibilities or obligations of that relationship, profession, or organization. I believe employees in a commerce setting may be dedicated and committed, and additional words to describe them could be "industrious" (hardworking) and "diligent" (showing care and thought in work activities).

Commerce employees, or those subject to at-will employment, do not take an oath of loyalty and therefore should not be considered loyal to these types of organizations. I believe this because I have been in company meetings where the employees were thanked for being loyal to the organization. As I heard the word "loyal" used, I would look around the room and watch the life drain further from their already stressed-out and exhausted faces because they have just been told they now have a loyalty to the organization, implying in a subtle way that they have more skin in the game than they really do.

I also disagree with the old saying "Sticks and stones may break my bones, but words can never hurt me." Broken bones can heal, and bones do not connect people to organizations. Words can linger in an employee's consciousness and cause long-term pain and resentment, and like internal injuries, the consequences are often not known until a more serious condition develops.

So be wise with your words and remember that silence is always better than hurried or ill-considered thoughts. Heider said, "The wise leader speaks rarely and briefly . . . no other outpouring goes on and on. It rains and then it stops. It thunders and then it stops. The leader teaches more through being than doing. The quality of one's silence conveys more than long speeches" (1985, p. 58). If you do not know the answer or need to think about your response, say you will get back to them later—then just make sure you do.

Motivation and Engagement

The last part of this chapter is a brief discussion on change, motivation, engagement, and balance in an organization. As a servant leader you have the awesome responsibility and goal to raise up and inspire all people you interact with. But, as a lead or supervisor, one day you may be given the daunting task by your boss to improve the motivation of your reports. Yes, this can happen. *Life and leadership moment: My opinion on motivation is it is like an employee who has an issue being tardy to work. You may try to adjust the start time to accommodate but soon realize the employee continues to be tardy. Tardiness is not solved by changing hours; the problem is psychological, and changing start times only shifts the problem to a later hour. If a person truly wants to be somewhere at a certain time, they will find a way to be there. Therefore, true motivation comes only from within (E. F. Johnson, personal conversation, November 22, 2017).*

Although there are many ways to motivate people, I believe there are two key internal motivators that can drive change in life and leadership: dissatisfaction and excitement. The motivation when a project or idea begins is like the fizz from a freshly opened soda can. But if the right type or amount of internal motivation is not driving the change, then, like an opened soda, the fizz soon fades, and the motivation goes stale.

The first key motivator, dissatisfaction, I learned from a guest speaker at a Servant Leader Cities Tour who had just published a book about employee engagement. The guest speaker was Joseph Patrnchak, who was the chief human resources officer for the Cleveland Clinic, and in my opinion, wrote one of the best field guides currently in print for effecting organizational change. He begins Chapter 4 of his book with the statement, "Real change starts with real dissatisfaction" (2016, p. 21). In the personal realm, I relate this statement to the dissatisfaction that drove my desire to end my cigarette addiction. During the decades I smoked, I often used smoking as a convenient escape strategy, but as I got older the escape turned into imprisonment, and the convenience turned into an annoyance and ruse. This realization and acknowledgment of my dissatisfaction was the catalyst that gave me the motivation, will power, and determination to end my addiction. In this case, and as is true so often, dissatisfaction was a powerful motivation tool that really worked.

The second motivator comes from the opposite extreme and is called excitement. Excitement generates anticipation, enthusiasm, and eagerness. Excitement makes people more likely to act because it taps into and awakens their spirit. Excitement can be the aftereffect of dissatisfaction, or it may originate from a long-needed change or a new idea. We can use the example of going on a vacation to show how a new idea can produce excitement and change, and how it relates to achieving a goal.

First, you realize the need for a change (motivation toward a goal). Second, you decide where you want to go (begin with the end in mind). Third, you figure out the logistics. Do you have the funds (budget) to go, what is the best and fastest route or type of transportation needed to get there (logistics), and who will go with you (human capital)? You put your plan in place, and you are on your way (execution). When you get to your vacation destination, you enjoy the perks of achieving your goal (celebration). After you return home you think about what could have been done differently or better to increase your relaxation and enjoyment for the next vacation (reflection). So, both dissatisfaction and excitement are powerful internal motivators that can be used to tap into the achievement of a goal.

It is true that most frontline jobs lack excitement, which is a demotivator, so finding a way to create excitement will be discussed later in this chapter. It is also true that many of the people I have encountered over my lifetime say their workplaces have an overabundance of dissatisfaction, so why then is motivation and change in such a short supply? A popular catchphrase in the early 2000s was "the struggle is real," and the motivation struggle is as real today as it has been for years past.

Clinical psychologist and influencer of management and motivational theory Frederick Herzberg, who created the well-known hierarchy of needs theory, confirms what I have seen and experienced. He says, "Motivator factors that are intrinsic to the job are: achievement, recognition for achievement, the work itself, responsibility, and growth or advancement. . . . The Hygiene factors extrinsic to the job include: company policy and administration, supervision . . . working conditions, salary, status" (2008, n.p.).

The motivators of dissatisfaction and excitement, along with Herzberg's motivators, originate from the internal needs and desires of a person. The Hygiene motivators are more like a temporary satisfier. Take salary for instance. Maybe you have heard employees complain that they are not paid enough for what they are expected to do. The Hygiene motivator of a salary increase will only motivate for a short time. After the positive effect of a raise wears off employees will return to their previous emotional state. Edward Johnson said in class one day that "a pay raise is a hygiene because it is like washing your hands; you need to keep repeating, giving, and raising the amount to get the same result."

If employees become too dependent on the extrinsic rewards, there is the possibility they will focus less on, or forget about, the intrinsic rewards. So knowing the difference between motivators and satisfiers can help you with the task of helping others find their internal motivation. You can also think about it this way: say you were trying to motivate a volunteer, family member, or significant other to do something difficult or perform an unfavorable task. Which motivator would you choose, and how would you go about doing it without having access to a carrot (a reward) or a stick (negative consequences for poor behavior)? Surely, it would be finding a way to motivate by one's passions, potentials, or abilities to achieve a desired goal.

Along with employees feeling overworked and underpaid is the pressure to do more with fewer people and resources, which I have seen as a constant struggle and demotivator between employees and employers. At times it may seem like your organization is on a roller-coaster ride: business picks up, the organization hire some temps; people leave the organization, sometimes they are replaced and sometimes not; business slows down, hiring freezes and cross-training becomes prevalent. Staffing an organization is a complex task, but the explanation is simple and is best explained by my professor, Edward Johnson, who used the fairy tale "Goldilocks and the Three Bears."

Organizations have a constant struggle between having not enough, too many, and just the right amount of staff, inventory, and services. Management will look into their proverbial crystal ball to decipher what the future of the business may be to make their best prediction about the future using the known and unknown factors of the economic environment. They need to attempt to preserve a solid workforce base to keep the organization functioning. There is much riding on these decisions; for instance, the need to retain employees, the risk of overhiring, and then the possibility and negative effects (for those who go and those who stay) of laying off those employees.

Even though it is a hardship and struggle to work shorthanded, you can help the employees realize their jobs are more secure because of it. Try sharing this perspective to keep motivation on track until the next climb of the roller coaster when the business begins to hire again. Of course, the opposite of this scenario can happen as well. Employees who feel overworked and/or lack CPR #1 (see p. 43) can always choose to vote with their feet. But even before attempting to help inspire and motivate employees, it is important to judge their true level of engagement. In an organization there may be employees who run the spectrum between being actively engaged, engaged, not engaged, and actively disengaged.

Richard Kyte said in a classroom lecture that it is the actively engaged through the not engaged employees that can swing back and forth between these categories at different times, but the actively disengaged employee will likely stay in that category. An employee in this stage will often undermine the organization and become like a virus that attempts to infect the other employees. Any attempt at motivation for this type of employee would be futile because engagement in and at an organization is based on the amount of social capital and the levels of trust as discussed earlier (see p. 35). My belief is it is better to help the actively disengaged employee find happiness with a different organization.

A final thought before we move on is the fallacy our culture tells us about work–life balance. Author Justine Musk's research unearthed a forgotten observation of life and work, reminding us that "the life/work balance was originally a term that anthropologists used in the 1800's . . . and their conclusion was that the thinner the line between what you did for work, and what you did for the rest of your life, the happier you were . . . so it wasn't about balance, it was about integration" (2016). Servant leaders are needed to help people understand this essential conclusion. A lot of employees may not realize this, and they may be stuck in a world where they are trying to balance an unhappy work life by adding more happiness to home life, or the workaholic with a bad home life is trying to balance that with more dedication to work. Either attempt is futile because it leaves one depending on an external, rather than internal, source to provide serenity.

You may have also heard the saying, "You do not have to like someone to work with them, just keep it professional." There will always be times when people just can't get along, but this statement can be damaging because it only furthers the divide between work and life integration. Would you want to go into work every day when you did not like anyone and just kept all your relationships strictly professional? How long would you want to, or be able to, stay in that type of environment?

A lot of frontline jobs do repetitive tasks that don't offer much for inspiration, so the simple saving grace is to have a work community that will help and support each other. Granted, not everyone is going to get along all the time, but when you create a community environment it goes a long way toward making a workplace where people have less dread when entering the building.

Although this section briefly discussed change, motivation, engagement, and balance in an organization, you may have also had a chance to reflect on yourself and how you may deal with these situations, and this is all part of becoming more self-aware and having the capability to understand yourself.

Understanding the Self

"The middle path for servant leaders is to avoid the extremes of either being driven by an out-of-control ego that has power and does harm . . . or creating a blissful self that expresses peace and harmony but is ineffectual in the real world" (Spears 1998, p. 273).

We discussed earlier that leaders take the middle of the road concerning trust, but we also stand in the middle of the road when it comes to the use of power and position. The quote above allows us to reflect on ourselves and ask questions such as, how much ego and power does harm? Is it more ego than power, more power than ego, or a specific combination of the two? How can one be fair and equitable when mixing personal style with organization culture and policy?

These few questions can make leadership appear to be a more difficult task when considering the different needs and perceptions of people, the current climate and culture, and what is expected from the leader. The extremes of power, harm, and being ineffectual are easier to identify, but when we think of the gray areas of leadership as in the questions in the previous paragraph, it is the subtle things we do (or do not do) daily that may gradually build up and weigh heavier on our followers—just like the proverbial straw that broke the camel's back.

To understand ourselves, it is important to know that our basic leadership and followership skills and traits come from our families or those who raised us, and the experiences we had growing up. For instance, when you were young you may have hung out at a friend's house and observed how their family's rules and structure differed from your own. I remember some families being stricter and others more lenient than my own, and I would use the experience of my family's structure to judge them on what I believed was the right and best way.

These basic emotions and perceptions from our upbringing carry on inside of us throughout our lives, and when we become leaders we incorporate our upbringing into how we approach and deal with people and situations. For instance, we tend to parent as we were parented, and lead as we have been led by others. But in being a leader, we need to elevate our decision-making beyond these basic beginnings, and adjust our approach and styles to make our leadership encompass a wider spectrum of views, perceptions, and cultural differences. An important part to making unselfish decisions is understanding how our ego may influence us.

Ego

Some people need things to be internalized before they are understood; for example, that is how I gained a better understanding of ego and how it affected my decision-making process as a leader. I found one of many privileges of attending college on the opposite side of my state was the three-and-a-half-hour drive there on Friday mornings, and then back home on Saturday evenings. This long drive provided ample amounts of time for reflection. One Saturday my class performed an exercise called "ego anonymous" where each student was asked to reflect on something we did, something we should have done, or something we could have handled differently, or, in some area of our lives where we were making excuses and justifying to ourselves why something happened.

Each student then stood up and gave an example of their self-centeredness. The examples ranged from the simple, such as taking over the remote control for the TV when they came home, to the moderate, such as always having the last word in conversations, to the more personal and private, where tears were shed. I had trouble coming up with an example on the spot, but I became aware of my ego and how it changes me a few hours later when I was driving home.

On that drive I came upon road construction. The highway was down to one lane for five miles, and as Murphy's Law dictates, I ended up behind the only car that drove ten miles an hour under the posted construction-zone speed limit. I immediately felt helpless with no way out from behind that driver, and powerless because there was no way to change my situation. I did the quick calculation in my mind and concluded I would be gaining an extra ten-plus minutes on my already long trip. Not a really big deal in hindsight, but at the moment and at beginning of my trip, it seemed like an eternity.

Obscenities spewed out of my mouth at this inconvenience as if my glasses were repeatedly sliding down my nose. And it was at that moment that something clicked inside of me, and I internalized what ego was. It was all about me and my wants. I wanted to get home as fast as possible, and my want was the only thing that mattered. I believed and expected all other drivers to know and not interfere with my plan. We all may assume other drivers know and abide the gray areas or unwritten rules of the highway; for example, go with the flow, if you want to drive slower use the right lanes, and if a driver looks in the rearview mirror and sees a long line of cars behind them in a construction zone, it most likely means they are the cause of the backup, so they should either speed up or pull over.

And here is the hypocritical part of that last sentence: I was expecting that slow driver to be thinking of other drivers' wants—specifically mine—while I was just thinking about myself and not considering the reasons why the driver ahead of me was driving that way. *Life and leadership moment: understanding the ego, and how to notice and control it when it shows itself, is a great benefit that can save you and others a lot of trouble and hurt. Know that understanding this is not a one-time fix, but something to be aware of for the rest of your life.*

I'll share something that recently happened to me that shows how ego can affect one's decision-making process. On a Friday, after a long and difficult week, I decided to stay late for the carrier pickups so my reports could leave work on time and start their weekend. All but one carrier picked up by closing time, and while I waited for this last carrier, I felt myself getting more hungry and tired. The last truck arrived a half hour later. I knew this driver well and we had established a great relationship over the years.

Usually, after backing the truck up to the dock, the driver would be out of the cab and ringing the doorbell right away. When this did not happen, I turned on the security camera to watch for the driver to walk up. As I watched and waited, then waited some more, I saw no movement. I became a bit more upset as each additional minute passed. After about ten minutes of waiting, I could feel myself starting to grow angrier, and then

I realized it was my ego running the conversation in my head instead of listening to or thinking rational thoughts.

I then made the decision to step out of my ego and ask myself if this was a normal behavior from the driver. My answer was no, the driver had never done this before. So I then asked myself what could be keeping him from coming out of the truck. I thought it could be a medical emergency, or maybe the driver had gotten a phone call with some bad news. By shifting the focus from my wants to having concern for him, I was able to make a drastic change in my attitude and emotions.

At that moment the doorbell rang, and as I let the driver in I immediately asked if he and everything was okay. The driver said everything was fine. He told me that as he was backing into the dock he had gotten a phone call from his Realtor up north where he would be retiring soon. A house had just come up for sale that was not listed on the market yet, and he was making plans to travel for the weekend to go see it. I told him I had been concerned and began to worry that something bad happened because of his delay, and that I was glad everything was okay. I could tell the driver was grateful that I had been concerned for him, and I hate to imagine what would have happened if I had let my ego control the situation. If I had had a bad attitude and expressed my ill feelings when the driver came in the door, it could have resulted in an unhappy start to the weekend for both of us, and possibly caused permanent damage to our long-term relationship.

These two examples of how our egos can dictate what we think, feel, and believe of our first impressions show that the characteristics of the ego are often generated by our own auto-pilot system, a system that can create its views and conclusions based on our biases, past experiences, and future expectations. Gilbert says that

> decades of research suggests that when it comes to collecting and analyzing facts about ourselves and our experiences, most of us have the equivalent of an advanced degree in Really Bad Science. . . . We accomplish this by unconsciously cooking the facts and then consciously consuming them. The dinner is in the dining room but the chef is in the basement. The benefit of all this unconscious cookery is that it works; but the cost is that it makes us strangers to ourselves. (2006, pp. 180–192)

This reasoning explains why I appeared as a stranger to myself during that brief road-rage incident. Chef Ego was in my basement preparing a meal called self-interest soufflé. I had been eating that meal for a long time and had given up paying attention to whether it tasted good or bad, or even if I could have made other choices from the menu. But our inner chef also has inside information on us, and likes to sneak us tasty treats to feed our ego.

The problem with this chef is if we are not regularly checking our refrigerator or cabinets for any rotten or expired ingredients, we may end up serving these treats to our guests.

The "treats" I'm referring to come most often from lack of CPR #1 (see p. 43). Servant leaders can also be affected by the lack of CPR #1 because we are human and have emotions too. But if we remain aware of the ego and recognize when negative emotions arise, we can become more self-aware and better understand our feelings and why we are having them. In addition, we must remember that leaders are being watched on a continuous basis, and the emotions we display will transfer to others. Jerald Greenburg, who is an author and senior psychologist at the Rand Corporation's Institute for Civil Justice writes that the technical term for this is "emotional contagion," which occurs when "the emotions we display tend to be picked up by others, resulting in a convergence of emotions. This . . . occurs regularly in the workplace, where emotions are easily spread" (2012, p. 146).

The authors of the book *Connected* add that "emotions spread from person to person because of two features of human interaction: we are biologically hardwired to mimic others outwardly, and in mimicking their outward displays, we come to adopt their inward states" (Christakis and Fowler 2009, p. 37). It is these inward states that leaders must be aware of when we first sense them affecting us. They are most commonly anger, embarrassment, shame, guilt, taking blows to our pride, and so forth, and are often the result of conflicts or disagreements we have with others.

When these emotions arise within us, they can lead to the second states of feelings, which are insecurity, worry, hate, jealousy, and revenge, to name a few. Chef Ego likes to feed us these secondary emotions also, so we need to be aware of this second stage and recognize and stop being served when the first state of emotions are being felt. At this point, it is important that we step back, take a breath, and remember the purpose of servant leadership; who we are serving and why we are serving them.

Reflection

When we notice emotions beginning to surface, that is our cue to refocus either on the problem, the person, or both. Our goal is to take ourselves out of the equation, which is always easier said than done, and reflection can help us get better at this task. In our fast-paced work lives, we become accustomed to making decisions on the fly and not thinking about long-term consequences. Without frequent reflection, you might very well be creating a reality show called *Workplace Nightmares*, and you as the leader could be the star of the show. The authors of the book *Authentic Conversations* observe that "through genuine, deep reflection, you are better equipped to confront uncomfortable truths about yourself. You are more prepared to shed unconscious assumptions about who you are, who others are, and what we want to create or accomplish together" (Showkeir and Showkeir 2008, p. 157).

While reflection is a powerful tool, it is not always easily accomplished. I have often tried to set aside time for reflection and contemplation while at work but ultimately found it too hard to disconnect from my tasks and surroundings. My opinion on reflection is that for it to be successful one must be able to focus on something completely different, or perform a menial task separate from the issue at hand, which frees one up to contemplate and think freely.

If you have ever come up with the perfect answer or comeback after a conversation has ended, you know what I'm talking about. If you have ever found the solution to a problem or issue while taking an eight-minute shower, you know what I'm talking about. When I used to run for exercise, I discovered and would always tell others that if I could not find the answer to my problems while running, there probably was not an answer to be found. Unlike our current society's focus on instant change and gratification, true reflection takes time, like going for a long run, or separation from the situation, like taking an eight-minute shower. So don't beat yourself up for not being able to solve issues while in the moment.

Leaders who make time for reflection will find that it is a two-part process. First, reflection can assist the leader to discover self-awareness, which can help them become more conscious of their character, feelings, motives, and desires through self-discovery. Second, being more self-aware can elevate the understanding of the self, and lead to the unearthing and the pursuit and fulfillment of talents and potentialities. Self-awareness opens the leader to self-actualization, which leads to the desire to fulfill external and selfless goals such as giving of yourself to help others realize their uniqueness, lessen their struggles, and help them to fulfill their potential—all qualities of the servant leader.

For example, through self-reflection I discovered a personal bias that was affecting my leadership and my reports—a bias that I was unaware of, but an important one. My bias came in the form of the self-fulfilling prophecies of the Pygmalion and Golem effects. Greenburg defines these two prophecies as the "Pygmalion effect—[managers have] positive expectations—[and give employees] emotional and professional support—[employees get] added experience and boosted confidence—[the result is] good performance. The Golem effect—[managers have] negative expectations—[and the employees have] emotional and professional support withheld—[employees get] limited experience and lowered confidence—[the result is] poor performance" (2012, p. 83).

Both prophecies fall under the trait of persuasion, and sometimes even a positive can have a negative side; let me explain how I was guilty of both. I mentioned earlier that people tend to gravitate toward the path of least resistance, and leaders are not exempt from this rule. When we get busy, it is human nature to find the fastest and most convenient way to achieve our daily goals rather than answer for our shortcomings the next day. When under pressure, leaders may use the path of least resistance and give the majority of projects to one or a select few employees they have confidence in to get the job done. This is what I was unintentionally doing.

Although our intent may be to complete the tasks and just make it through the day, we also risk introducing the following unintended negative effects that resemble a triple-edged sword. The first edge is that at first the employee getting all the tasks will feel the positives of the Pygmalion effect. The second edge is that same employee, who may be under pressure to perform daily duties, keeps getting the additional tasks and begins to view them as an obstacle rather a benefit. This can often lead the employee to feel frustration and resentment toward the leader and organization. Too much of a good thing is not a good thing.

The third edge is the Golem effect for the employees who do not get the chance to work on tasks or projects, and observe the select employees getting all the special projects, which projects favoritism and exclusion. If you are a new and emerging leader you may have experienced the first and second edges because being given additional duties and responsibilities is how most of us worked our way up to a leadership position. To get results, servant leaders strive to use persuasion instead of their authority and coercion, but we must also be careful because persuasion can come in forms other than verbal.

A fortunate and easy solution we have to avoid these self-fulfilling prophecies comes as a simple, three-letter word . . . *ask*. Just ask your other reports if they want the opportunity. If they turn it down at least they will have had the offer and a chance for the job and not feel left out or overlooked. And if they say yes, you just may be surprised at the talents you uncover. *Life and leadership moment: this is only one example of how developing a better understanding of the self can help improve the lives of others and yourself. The most important part of this example is that it shows us something that was not obvious, that things we do not know about ourselves can be affecting our life, the lives of others, and our leadership.*

Life and leadership is a continuous improvement project, and one should always be seeking ways to better the mind, body, spirit, and soul. Poet and author David Whyte writes about the oxymoron of employees bringing their souls into the workplace. He said,

> Preserving the soul means that we come out of hiding at last and bring more of ourselves into the workplace. Especially the parts that do not "belong" to the company. In a sense, the very part of us that doesn't have the least interest in the organization is our greatest offering to it. . . . We are not our job descriptions, and the small, confining prisons those descriptions have made for us. . . . As the Chinese sage Wu Wei Wu admonished: "Why are you unhappy? Because 99.9% of what you think, and everything you do, is for yourself, and there isn't one." (1994, pp. 292–294)

Professor and clinical psychologist Jordan Peterson said, "You can only find out what you believe [rather than what you think you believe] by watching how you act. You simply don't know what you believe, before that. You are too complex to understand yourself. . . . It takes careful observation, and education, and reflection, and communication with others, just to scratch the surface of your beliefs" (2018, p. 101). Therefore, understanding the self is a personal quest that is driven by the desire and commitment to growth of the individual to in turn better effect the growth of others and the community. This is another servant leader trait: commitment to the growth of people.

My perspective of servant leaders is that they have the responsibility for carrying and passing on their inner fire of goodness, just like the thousands of torch bearers for the Olympic Games. Servant leaders are not concerned about personal greatness, but rather that their inner fire, *their spirit*, is sparked inside to help illuminate another's torch. These fires will only light when the internal roots of the leader, and the roots of the relationships in and out of the workplace, grow from a more secure foundation. This foundation is seeded not from changing people or situations by correcting or using coercion but rather from a healing mindset, and when leaders come to terms with their own selves, they can begin to grow into maturity.

CHAPTER 4

Maturity

Maturity is the phase of growth where the tree grows bigger and begins to focus on procreation.

"My life is like a loan given from God, and I will give this loan back, but with interest" (Belic 2011, 1:10:06).

Spirit

I believe a key reason leadership is so difficult to teach and learn is because effective leadership is like an art form, and art is only created through practice that is driven by inspiration and desire that comes by way of our spirit. Greenleaf said, "The danger, perhaps, is to hear the analyst too much and the artist too little. . . . The spirit (not knowledge) is power . . . if only the spirit could be aroused" (2002, p. 25). We have all perhaps felt the analytical effects of our work life, and may have wondered about that paradoxical notion that why only our body is of value while our spirits are left to waste. If spirit could be infused into our work, our minds and bodies would once again become energized, internal motivation would be sparked, creativity would flow like a fast-flowing river. Could you imagine how much more productive and engaged employees would be, and how that would translate into happy customers?

Our spirit is the magnetic part of us that helps point the needle of our internal compass to true north. When I engage my spirit at work, I somehow become a better leader; I give more and better attention to my reports and projects. Ego steps out of the equation because I pay less attention to what others are doing and focus more on my inner drive and strength. When the spirit is disengaged the ego can conjure up negative feelings of worry, anger, frustration, and jealousy that stem from focusing on the lack the of CPR #1 (see p. 43), and then longing for the weekend is our only saving grace. Whyte said, "We . . . spend too much time and have too much psychic and emotional energy invested in the workplace for us to declare it a spiritual desert bereft of life-giving water. The belief has been that we can drink only on weekends or vacations. . . . Life does not seem to be impressed . . . that we can ignore our deeper desires because we happen to be earning a living" (1994, p. 69).

Organizations, like people, are complex, and the addition of diverse people into the mix multiplies the complexity exponentially. This makes the need for rules and structure important because these dictate the organization's culture. But inside of this complex mountain lies a gold mine of inspiration and engagement to be discovered. Best-selling author Joseph Marshall says, "Boundaries for function and behavior are important to any organization that wants to be successful; but inspiration for the heart and the spirit should be important too. Because inspiration lends itself to the achievement of goals and objectives, inspirational leadership is as necessary for success as oxygen is for breathing" (2009, p. 292). And inspiration is the catalyst of spirit that helps to transcend normal day-to-day activities into higher purposes and accomplishments.

The human body is similar in some respects to an organization, as the total health of both depend on the mind, body, and spirit. It is no coincidence that roots of the word "organization" refer to the "act or process of organizing, the arranging of parts into an organic whole" (Etymonline 2021). We may all agree that if the *mind* is troubled by something it can affect the body and spirit. For example, if someone is told repeatedly they are useless they may begin to believe it, and their body and spirit can react negatively. If your *body* has ever decided to give you that special-occasion zit on your face, you may become self-conscious at an event and withhold your personality from revealing your true, normal, and socially interactive self, and this can affect your mind and spirit. If someone finds out their significant other has been cheating on them their *spirit* and zest for life may decline and then everything in the world is viewed in a negative light, and the mind and body react to a whirlwind of undesirable and negative emotions.

For an organization to achieve its organic wholeness, the three aspects of mind, body, and spirit must also be aligned with its why, what, and how. Kyte describes this as the mind (why) leading body (what) and spirit (how). The *why* consists of the organization's mission, its goal or purpose . . . something that provides meaning for all those who have a stake in the organization. . . . The *what* consist of the organization's . . . people, buildings, financial assets . . . and so on. The *how* consists of the organization's power . . . whatever the organization does intentionally or unintentionally to direct the way things get done. (2016, p. 63)

From my experience one of the greatest demotivators in the workplace is the failure of an organization to connect its purpose to their employee's spirit, and the employee's failure to find their spirit's place in their job or the organization. Although there are many reasons neither happen, there are three sides that need to be discussed. The first side is that many employees don't come preprogrammed with, nor have they given much thought to (beyond the physical), the unique gift(s) they can offer the workplace and the world. I believe the main reason for this is poverty: not poverty in an economic sense, but poverty in the areas of opportunities, resources, and spirit.

Just like leadership theories, hiring theories, recruitment, and selection practices do well, but they can also provide unpredictable results. Although no one hiring process is perfect, the second side is one that a new and emerging leader may miss. An important part of the hiring process is to begin with the end in mind. For instance, consultant and human resources manager Amy Whittenberger said, "The responsibility of a leader should include preparing the direct reports for their next role. Even when you are hiring, look beyond the current role to imagine where this candidate will fit into the future of the organization" (personal conversation, March 22, 2021). This statement agrees with Greenleaf's best test of a servant leader, "Do those served grow as persons? Do they, while being served, become healthier, wiser, freer, more autonomous, more likely themselves to become servants?" (2002, p. 27).

Life and leadership moment: If we, as leaders are not helping our reports move up and out of our department, we are not doing our job for our reports, or our organization. If we are not helping our neighbors, friends, family members, or community to rise up and above to become better than they were yesterday, we are not performing our role in life as human beings.

The third side is said best by what my friend Keith Jones, who had a lifelong career in human resources management told me about hiring, "You don't know what you got until you get it in the boat. No matter what you got on the line you never know what will rise to the surface until you land the catch" (personal communication, March 21, 2021). When we first hear this statement we may reflect on past hires we thought would be a great fit, but later turned out not to be quite the right fit, or maybe they were the exact opposite of what we expected. We are then left wondering how we could have missed discovering this beforehand and how to prevent it from happening again. But what if we approach this quote from the perspective and the purpose of hiring the spirit? You may see the hiring process in a whole new light. Think about your current organization and reports. How much do we, as leaders, really know about the people we lead and the other people we work with?

Getting to know the people we lead and work with plays a major part in building community, which is another pillar of servant leadership. No matter how big or small your workplace is, it is a community. The word "community" is the combination of the two words, "common" and "unity" (Kyte, personal communication, March 23, 2018). Our job as leaders is to help create this common unity, and the first step in doing this is getting to know our coworkers (or neighbors) in a deeper and more personal way, and the easiest way to do that is to have authentic curiosity about them, and that can begin as early as the hiring process.

Having authentic curiosity for others helps leaders create community by developing social capital and bonding (see chapter 3). As we discover and build these bonds, social capital will become the superglue that binds people together in the workplace, and one result will be the discovery of the unique qualities, talents, and desires that people have. As these come to light, the leader can use them to elevate and bring forth the employees' spirits, and become the conduit that can create bridging capital to unite people through their commonality. I have witnessed employees who were at first distant to each other suddenly become connected by realizing a commonality between them, and through this bonding not only camaraderie increases but also productivity. The leader's job is to uncover potential that was previously unseen and unknown, which once revealed, can be used for growth and possibilities that would otherwise never have been brought to the surface.

What if you approached the spirit of your work community and reports as a blank canvas for painting, and the people and their gifts as the paint? The more colors (people's gifts) you have to choose from, the more elaborate, imaginative, and meaningful the end result will be. Unlike a one-dimensional picture, the painting a leader can create can use layer upon layer to build on to create a masterpiece. The question once again is how do we go about it? Just like how different colors of paint combine to create a painting, building community is the basic foundation of any company. Founder of the master of arts in servant leadership and distinguished professor Thomas Thibodeau said in class one day that the word "company" comes from two Latin words "'com' = 'with,' 'together'... + 'panis' = 'bread.'" In short, together, we break bread. When we invite company into our homes this definition makes total sense. When we apply the word to your organization does this definition share the same meaning?

I believe it could, and it should, but an unfortunate truth is that for many companies the cited meaning is far from a reality. When we take our breaks from the busyness of our day, we may see ourselves or our employees withdrawing into the voluntary and solitary confinement of offices, cars, or the internet as respite. We believe these brief retreats will provide us the separation and relief we seek from our busy and stressful day, but in doing it this way, are we really getting the respite we need? When we retreat into our private and isolated spaces, we are depriving ourselves of the most important and necessary practice that can alleviate our feelings of emptiness, loneliness, and seclusion—that is, companionship.

The simple act of eating together, or just sitting down to have a beverage and talk with others is possibly the easiest and most convenient way to counteract the stress of your day while simultaneously building common unity in your workplace. An easy way to build companionship is to arrange a potluck lunch. During an event like this you will see the dominant groups of people congregate, but also pay attention to the introverted people, and those on the margins of the group. Make a point to join and talk with them.

Look around and acknowledge to yourself when you see people sit with and speak to others whom they might not usually have contact with on a daily basis. You are witnessing the creation of bonding capital that can lead to bridging capital in the future (see p. 36). Your actions have sparked the fire of building community and companionship. Enjoy, and rejoice in the moment! *Life and leadership moment: How can you make treats even sweeter? It is important to understand that if you bring in treats for the team it is only a short-term satisfier to improve morale. Like trying free samples at the grocery store it becomes a hygiene-type satisfier where you need to keep giving more to achieve the same result. When leaders connect the treats to a person, group or achievement, a specific purpose, event, or celebration, the intent of the treat is not only appreciated in the moment, but it can also become an intrinsic motivator for future behavior.*

If you cannot find a specific reason for the treats, you have creative freedom to make up your own holiday or original occasion, like an "assembler appreciation day" or "thank you for all you do day." Remember that you always get more of what you acknowledge, and people need to be affirmed that they matter. Thibodeau said, "By celebrating what is right we find the energy to fix what is wrong" (personal communication, November 17, 2018). When you have a deeper knowledge of your employees' lives, it will help you celebrate what is important to them and give them more support. And in knowing your employees, and creating community, you are building room for spirit.

Learning what is important to your reports and other employees helps that become important to you, and you can be the conduit that helps that become important to others. Something as simple as a good luck or sympathy card or a baby shower (for a man or a woman) can go a long way toward showing the employees that you, the organization, and others care about them, that we all can share in, and care about, each other's high and low moments in life. I know my words may sound overly optimistic, or may appear to be as useless as a bicycle is to a fish when applying them to your own organization, but keep in mind that it is in those instances when community may be needed the most.

If you have been in an unfavorable environment for any length of time, you run the risk of becoming acclimated to that environment. Journalist, author, and public speaker Malcolm Gladwell said, "To the worm in horseradish, the world is horseradish" (2007). It is easy to become accustomed to, and then develop an immunity to an environment. The longer you are in that environment the more you risk developing tunnel vision regarding your processes, values, and ethics. Regardless of what type of organization you are involved in, there is always one common denominator, and that is the human factor. If you are in a negative environment, one of the hardest things you as a new and emerging leader may struggle with is trying to keep, and project, a positive outlook, even when you yourself know, feel, and struggle to fight the negativity that exists inside and around you. Former senior executive in the Veterans Health Administration Linda Belton tells the story of Pollyanna, which offers a fresh perspective to help us through these trying times.

> Do you remember the children's story of Pollyanna? Pollyanna is an orphan taken in by her reclusive aunt. Despite a difficult life, she always looks for the positive; searches for the best in people. Conversely, her aunt always expects the worst and has a low estimation of human nature.
>
> Events escalate until Pollyanna's brightness is finally extinguished by the persistent negativity around her. With her light gone, family and townsfolk acknowledge how empty their lives

have become. Of course there's a happy ending when the community "culture" shifts to adopt Pollyanna's optimism.

It has always baffled me to hear the derisive tone associated with "being a Pollyanna." What does it say about a society where cynicism has a higher value than idealism? Where a cheerful, hopeful approach is seen as unrealistic or flaky? Where caring is overridden by judging? Where learning about someone's failure is more satisfying than hearing of their success? Where we seek to define our separateness more than our connection? . . .

We are faced daily with life's tough realities, things we don't like, events beyond our control, even pain. It's not unnatural to become jaded, frustrated, demoralized. But perhaps there has never been a time that we needed Pollyanna's more. (2016, pp. 21–22)

This brief quotation does more to encapsulate what department leads and supervisors experience and struggle with on a daily basis than anything I've come across. One of the most difficult things for us to do as leaders is to keep a positive attitude in times of distress. We often face the ongoing problem of how we can keep another's ice cream cold when our own internal heat has melted our treat and motivation. How do we show, project, and convince others that the world is not horseradish when we are living in the same environment? The answer is never easy, but this is where community, creativity, continuous learning, and spirit combine to help us through our moments of doubt and uncertainty.

One last thought about spirit. Some time ago I heard a quote from English poet Cecil Baxter that stuck with me: "You don't get anything clean without getting something else dirty" (2015). After reading this quote I bet you're now thinking about the things you clean and where that dirt goes. Like when washing dishes, the sponge gets dirty, or when cleaning a carpet, the water turns dark. But when I started to think about the spirit, in addition to the soul, I could not think of one way when a person cleans their spirit that it transfers its dirt onto another, and in contrast, if a clean spirit helps another to clean theirs, both spirits will remain clean.

Isn't it amazing that spirit is the only force in the universe that defies this logic? For any organization, family, or community to not tap into this powerful and abundant force is an unfortunate loss for all. The human spirit is powerful, but so is our ability to make mistakes and let emotions take control over our judgments and words. When we act or react from the ego instead of the spirit, we risk transferring our dirt onto others. One of the best ways to keep one's spirit engaged is through continuous learning, which grows our self-awareness and helps us to become better servants and leaders.

Learn, Lead, Serve

Life and leadership moment: If at first you do not succeed, please try, try, try, and try again. Even when we feel like throwing in the towel, we need to remember we can, and should, rely on others to help us in our times of distress. And when it feels like we're supporting the world solely on our own shoulders, that is because we have made it so.

The term "servant leader" is an intentional oxymoron, and being a servant leader is one of the hardest things one can undertake. Every day is a paradox, like starting over while continuing at the same time. Servant leadership is being involved in others' lives, which goes beyond the workplace to being truly concerned and willing to help people with the many difficulties of life. In doing so, you may find yourself frustrated, angry, scared, troubled, and exhausted, but you may also enjoy some of the greatest highs and feelings of satisfaction and happiness. You could have these same emotions if you were not practicing servant leadership, but in taking the servant leader path, the meaning behind what you are doing, the relationships you create and sustain, and the end results you have your hand in creating will make your journey more worth your investment.

Of course, we all get paid to do our jobs, but there are real tangible and intangible differences when the heart is applied in leadership. I'm sure you have seen or felt the difference in care or service when a provider is only in it for the paycheck. Would you rather be fed by a chef who cares more about quantity than quality? Would you rather see a doctor who looked at you as a number rather than an individual, or work for an employer with the same mindset? Would you rather your reports follow you because they have to, or because they want to? You can probably feel and relate to these variances more after reading that last sentence and reflecting on your own team and organization.

You may be able to look back on your life to find examples of people who selflessly helped you achieve something. For me, I look to my mother. She was a German-born citizen who married an American military officer, and then came on a boat by herself to America. She taught herself English and found a career in physical therapy. When I was in first grade, I was falling behind my classmates in reading. My mother made the decision that she was going to help me succeed. She had my best interests in mind, and with her selfless help, by the end of the school year I was at the top percentage of my class for reading.

My mother's selfless sacrifice is a prime example of what a servant leader's purpose, goal, and desire to help others entails. Servant leaders have the selfless objective of helping others to realize, reach, and achieve their goals, and this reach is not limited to outside relationships. Servant leaders continuously search for what they do not know, and seek to build on their own knowledge to give themselves the opportunity for internal growth to better effect their internal and external world.

To keep the fires of our reports and others burning, we need to find ways to continuously fuel our own fires. The leadership style you create comes first from discovering your own art and craft. While teaching me one day, my music teacher and lifelong friend Paul Tadder said that "I can't make you creative. I can only give you the tools to help you be creative. And what you do with these tools is up to you" (P. Tadder, personal communication, March 7, 1999). In many ways servant leadership is related to learning a musical instrument because both consist of learning the fundamental theory and physical aspects, and having an inner purpose that drives motivation.

When learning an instrument we begin with the fundamentals of inspiration, putting in the practice time with the end result of mastery as our goal. Then we apply our new understanding and learning to build on our previous knowledge and expand our techniques. Both fundamentals and desire to achieve are fueled by our purpose and yearning to create. Then it is practice, practice, and more practice. Practice causes growth, and as we grow we eventually begin to incorporate other styles, techniques, and genres into our repertoire. These all lead to our path on the way to mastery of the instrument.

You may know of, or have heard of musicians who, after a successful career, decide to return to their roots, or go back to the basics, to rediscover themselves and the original love that attracted them to music. There could be many reasons why a musician would do this, but they most likely evolve from what my music teacher and I discussed about music theory during a lesson. He told me that "you can only take music theory so far until you come back around again to the basics" (P. Tadder, personal communication, March 14, 1999). Leadership is no different. Life can become complicated and complex. Sometimes servant leaders need to remember to return back to the basics of the philosophy: who are we serving and why?

You may have heard about the Penrose stairs, but if you haven't let me briefly explain. It is an illusion originally created by Oscar Reutersvärd and then enhanced by Lionel and Roger Penrose. In the illusion, if you walk the staircase in one direction it appears you would always be descending, and if walk in the opposite direction you would always be ascending. And in figure 1 we will be concerned only with the positively ascending aspect.

Figure 1. Knowing-and-Growing-the-Self Triangle

Figure 1 describes the Knowing-and-Growing-the-Self Triangle. Just like a person ascending the Penrose stairs, we as leaders need to remain in a constant and ascending loop of continuous learning and growth. This may sound like a chore, but if we approach it from an artist's point of view, the task can be enjoyable and spirit renewing. At the bottom of the triangle we find ourselves where we were yesterday, or where we are today. This is our baseline of being self-reliant in our current skills, abilities, judgments, resources, and environment. Then suddenly an event happens in our lives that changes our perceptions of reality, challenges our fixed beliefs, or is something we just do not have an easy answer for.

We then move up to the next stage of the triangle called self-awareness. Because servant leaders care about doing the right thing for others and/or ourselves, we begin to search for resources or information that will guide us onto the right path for decision-making, and not the path of least resistance. We become more conscious of our own character, feelings, motives, desires, and biases. We begin a new journey in self-reflection and self-discovery. Along the way we discover information that elevates the understanding of ourselves, our environment, and our world. Sometimes self-awareness will also lead us to discovering talents, potentials, and inspirations that we never knew existed.

After becoming self-aware, we move up to the next stage, which is self-actualization. Using the new information and new understanding gained through thought and reflection, we come to realize our new potential and appreciation for ourselves and others. We gain a desire to share our new perspective with our community, and we place a higher value on the quality of the human spirit. We have a greater understanding of how our internal and external relationships, virtues, and life purpose work together to heal others to create wholeness and well-being. We treat people more as ends unto themselves, and have a renewed outlook on an individual's value, dignity, and worth.

Taking all of this in, we move up to the final stage of the triangle of self-regeneration. "The prefix re- means 'again,' and generate means 'to produce or bring into existence'" (Dictionary.com 2021). Much like how a starfish can regenerate one of its limbs, or even its entire body, servant leaders are open and willing to provide themselves with the chance and opportunity to regrow a small or large part of themself. Once this happens, the servant leader leaves the top of the triangle, but the tip of the triangle figuratively breaks the leader into two pieces.

Half flows down the left side of the triangle picking up the individual and the mind. The other half flows down the right to pick up the societal and body. Both halves fall to the bottom and pick up the organizational and spirit, and then come together once again in our new stage of self-reliance. This creates a new understanding of ourselves and the world, and a renewed belief in the goodness of humanity. Be cognizant of where you are in the triangle so you can reach the top and regrow yourself in your role as a leader.

Going through this process can be a life-changing event. When Greenleaf wrote that "awareness is not a giver of solace—it is just the opposite. It is a disturber and an awakener," (2002, p. 41), he must have been speaking from experience. The following example of going through the knowing-and-growing-the-self triangle certainly awoke and disturbed me, and it also helped both my life and leadership become better through contemplation and reflection, resulting in personal growth. Here is my triangle *life and leadership moment.*

Stage 1. Self-Reliance. Early in my career I reported to a manager whom I deemed to be more self-serving than serving. The traits in that manager I observed included self-interest—for example, by withholding information for personal gain—and had what I would call "chameleon values"—values that would change with the situation to enhance self-worth and self-preservation: by not allowing or training others to move up and out of their positions to secure permanence in future positions. These actions were not everyday occurrences, but they did produce a gradual wearing down of trust for management and employee morale. I knew my tenure under this manager had an effect on me, but it was not until I reported to a different manager that I began to realize how much these actions had conditioned and influenced my own leadership style.

One morning at work, a customer complaint came in and this past manager blamed the error on my department. That in itself was not an issue, but what triggered my defenses was that I knew that my past manager was often guilty of committing the same type of error, but on a much larger scale. And now that I was no longer under his control, I wanted to expose this contradiction and get some form of retribution for similar past transgressions. I quickly gathered my evidence and went to protest to my new manager.

This type of behavior and attitude, getting retribution, was the baseline where I had become self-reliant. But when I approached my new manager with my protest and evidence, instead of joining me and feeding my fire, I was redirected and told that my current path was not going to make the situation better. The manager observed that I was engaging in a "you get me, and I'll get you" contest, that I should instead take responsibility for and correct my department's deficiency, and then think about a more positive way I could approach the larger issue. I agreed and went back to my daily duties, but with an additional sense of self-reflection and contemplation.

Stage 2. Self-Awareness. I knew my manager was right, and it was not long until I realized I had been reacting to similar situations in this way for some time. This was my self-reliant wake-up call, and this situation would be the catalyst for me to do the right thing for myself and others, to awaken myself and become more self-aware by challenging my fixed beliefs and perception of reality. As morning turned into noon, I began to recognize my reliance on this way of thinking. I asked myself how my words, actions, and thoughts were affecting others around or reporting to me. How much damage had I done that had been unnoticed until now? Thibodeau said during a classroom lecture, "You can't lead people past where you are." I was stuck in a self-imposed causality loop, and I knew I had to figure out how to escape from it.

After contemplating this issue all day, before I went home I thanked my manager for enlightening me and said I needed further contemplation to discover the root cause of my behavior. At home later that evening I was sitting outside by a fire, half paying attention to my issue and half reading a book. I put the book down to check what was happening on social media, and I saw someone had posted something interesting. The post asked readers to recall a favorite childhood memory, to respond in writing, and to describe that memory using as much detail as possible.

I put down my device and began to recall some of my favorite memories. At first many short-term memories were recalled, and then it seemed that I suddenly ran out of memories. This disturbed me for moment, but as I sat staring at the fire, more of my long-term and forgotten memories soon began to bubble up to the surface, many of which I had not thought about in a long, long time. Eventually a memory emerged from deep inside that brought forth joy at first, but would end in shame.

From the time I was born to about the middle of my third-grade school year, my family lived across the street from a family that had two brothers. One brother was my age, and the other was a few years older. Back in those days most children walked to and from school, as did I. But my trouble was that the older brother was a bully; if he did not find me before school to take my lunch money, he would be waiting for me somewhere on my long walk home after school. I would take different routes and try different times in an attempt to avoid him, but if he found me and I did not have any change to give him, I ended up paying with a beatdown. Although I was friends with the younger brother, the friendship wasn't as strong as it could have been because I often felt he often used me to practice his own bullying skills through rough play and play fighting.

When I was eight years old and in the middle of third grade my family was going to move to a new house. The night before we moved, the younger brother and I were playing catch with a football that he had borrowed from our school. I knew he did not know we were moving, so I used this opportunity to devise a sinister plan. I asked if I could keep the football overnight because I wanted to play with it a little longer. He said okay, as long as I gave it back to him the next day before school so he would not get in trouble with the school and his mother.

I realized I had a chance at retribution for my years of being bullied. I intentionally took that football under the false pretense of returning it the next day—which of course I never did. My family moved the next day and I never saw those brothers again. In the end payback was mine, and I finally got the upper hand and retribution for the angst suffered at the hands of those brothers. In my eight-year-old mind the end was justified by the means, but sitting and staring at the fire this night, I realized that the joy I got from this victory was turned into shame by how and what I did to achieve the end result.

Stage 3. Self-Actualization. It was at that instant I had a moment of clarity and the hair stood up on my arms. I said to myself, that's it! That's the root cause I was searching for! I made the connection between this memory and how I had been harboring these emotions and unconsciously carrying this affliction with me to the present day. *New York Times* columnist David Brooks once said that "pain that is not transformed gets transmitted" (2019). Because I had never transformed or come to terms with this pain from my past, I was still operating in the present using the same tactic; except in my current world the means to the end only resulted in a zero-sum game.

After a long weekend of contemplation, I gained a greater understanding of myself and how I could use this new realization to improve and heal. When I got back to work it was not long before I began to notice the effect my actions had on others. When I reacted to a situation with frustration and anger, I could now see how my words were affecting others' thoughts and actions, as the conversations reflected back by the employees were mirroring both. It became clear to me that my internal sourness had a much wider and more negative effect than I had originally thought. Here were folks who were depending on me to be a mentor and example, and my example was as obvious to me now as that special occasion zit. I guess the old adage is true, misery loves company, and my misery liked to have a full house. Instead of accepting things as they were and focusing on how to make things better, I often regressed back to complaining and venting my thoughts. But through thought and reflection I gained a new understanding of myself, and I made the decision to make a change to pursue the higher value of how I can help to heal myself and others.

Stage 4. Self-Regeneration. The process for starting over and regrowing myself came relatively quickly this time. I could now recognize and respond appropriately when I sensed the inclination toward retribution had been triggered in me, but I still needed work to bring into existence my new perspective and undo the harm I had done. I will probably never rid myself of this deep-seated tendency, but having realized how and why it is there is a big step toward healing myself. And when I notice similar words or emotions in another, I am better prepared to offer constructive advice, just as I was helped by my new manager.

So if you find yourself in this position, I feel it is proper now to return to the only advice I gave early on in this book, that is to *start with the heart*. When your intentions are true and noble you will be on the right path. The path will always have obstacles, but as long as you are willing to find your faults, improve yourself, and be open to change, opportunities will keep presenting themselves to you, and your life will not become stagnant. You might be thinking to yourself why you would need to do all this work on top of your already busy life, when every day feels like you are trying to drink from a firehose. But, servant leaders should not/cannot become stagnant in their growth. You have the awesome responsibility to be involved in people's lives and the privilege to make a difference for the better. You can clear the path for others to lead, and you need to see yourself as a leader no matter what you do, where you are, or how many times you may fail.

Life and leadership moment: if you neglect to use your gifts and talents they can end up working against you. Servant leaders heal people and want to guide and transform their lives, and you yourself will become transformed in the process. You will contemplate questions such as, "How did I become this way and why do I think that?" And as you help others find and express more meaning in their work and lives, the process can also affect you in different and unimagined ways—maybe by going deep and far enough inside yourself to consider making the hard choice between a purpose and a paycheck. The second half of the last Greenleaf quote (p. 73) fits well here, "Do they, while being served, become healthier, wiser, freer, more likely to become servants themselves? And what is the effect on the least privileged in society? Will they benefit or at least not be further deprived" (2002, p. 27)?

Self-care and satisfaction with yourself is just as important as what you do to help others. Notice I did not refer to happiness here. Happiness is subjective. For example, what made you happy when you were a child will not have the same effect when you're a teenager, and so on throughout your life. If you have ever lost something, and spent an abundant amount of time looking for it, I bet you have instead found that thing when you were looking for something else. This is not by accident, but rather how life works. Do not look for or pursue happiness; happiness occurs as a result of what you do. Helping and serving others is an easy and effective way to pay your life's loan back with interest.

When you set your sights on a noble goal, the goodness of life seeks you out instead of you searching for it. So remember, you are your own boss, and your own employee. How good a boss are you of you; are you setting goals and leading yourself? Are you providing the right means and discipline to achieve them? How good an employee are you? How well are you following your own directions and plans to achieve your goals? Professor and scholar Henry Mintzberg said in his book *Simply Managing*, "I don't want you to leave this book knowing. I want you to leave it, as I do, imagining, reflecting, questioning" (2013, p. 12). You know inside yourself what good can look and feel like, or what you foresee good is or is possible, so use that as your guideline to refine and rekindle your inner light as you learn and continue to grow.

There are no perfect leaders. Take that pressure off yourself now. Seek out honest feedback about your leadership, and welcome true judgment, as this is gold that you will not get from any other source—gold in the sense of waking you up to things you may not see or deficiencies you are not aware of. If your reports feel safe and comfortable enough to honestly tell you what you need to hear, not what they think you want to hear, that is a good clue you are on the right path. Servant leadership is not the path of least resistance, it is the path of most persistence in growth and change for all. When you truly know what is working and what is not, only then can you make real change for the better.

Every person has an artist inside. It does not matter what they are good or bad at today. Servant leaders look to find and grow whatever talent is there, and life has a magical way of growing toward the light when the light is revealed. If you have ever taught someone and they suddenly internalize that light, or when you see in their eyes that they actually get "it," and you see they grow that little bit in front of you, you understand what it feels like to be a servant leader. Therefore, the final *life and leadership moment is: always speak the truth with love.*

Be authentic with your reports, and they will be authentic back and there for you when you are in need. You have the power to change your world. You are the person you have been waiting for to initiate the change you know needs to happen. By inspiring a culture of trust and respect where employees feel cared for, empowered, valued, connected, protected, and respected, you will create a safe place that allows you access to be more involved in people's lives. When you are more involved in their lives, you have a better chance to coach others to be better servant leaders, and then you can pass the torch and others can become leaders and coaches themselves.

When we learn, we can lead. When we lead, we can serve. We will end as we began. I welcome you, the new and emerging servant leader, to your leadership arboretum.

Acknowledgments

I want to thank my family for their love and encouragement, especially my wife, Tabitha Osborne, for holding down the fort the many nights I was locked away writing; my daughter, Rebecca Osborne, for joining me on my trips to La Crosse and our many conversations on servant leadership; my sister, Karen Kong, for listening, guiding, and just being there when I needed to talk; and my brother-in-law, Rany Kong, who gave a long-haired kid an opportunity, and provided the example I would carry throughout my life.

I wish to express my deep appreciation to my best friends, Keith and Sue Jones, who selflessly and tirelessly offered their time and life experience to assist me with my writing, proofreading my stories and scripts, contemplating my ideas, and putting up with my Native American flute obsession.

I am most grateful to Rick Kyte and Thomas Thibodeau, my teachers, mentors, and friends who gave me the opportunity to be more than the sum of my parts; who believed in me and helped me to discover my why; who continue to inspire me through their goodness, wisdom, and vision;

and Viterbo University, who stood up for the servant leadership program that has and continues to improve lives and build communities.

A very special thanks to my coworkers, Phil Cwik, for being a friend, mentor, supporter, and a natural-born servant leader who continues to help me learn to better serve others; Richie Garcia, for our lunchtime talks, for the common unity, the chicken wings, and the camaraderie that helped me to keep my sanity on numerous occasions during some rough times; Randy Jones, for being a sounding board, sharing our grief and happiness, and helping me with and through his wisdom; Larry Perez, for the mentoring, challenging my preconceptions, and teaching me the right way to eat a tamale.

I am particularly indebted to the great folks at Fulcrum Publishing. I could not have hoped or wished for a better team to work with. Who would have thought that publishing a book could be such a fun, fulfilling, and uplifting experience? Even though I wrote the manuscript, I have no opposition to considering this *our* book. Thank you to:

Sam Scinta: Publisher

Alison Auch: Senior Editor

Kateri Kramer: Marketing Director

Patty Maher: Book and Video Production Manager

Miracles do happen, not when we are expecting them, but when good people get together and have fun creating something for the common good. This book is the proof that miracles do exist.

References

Baxter, C. 2015. "Forbes Quotes." Retrieved March 26, 2021, from
https://www.forbes.com/quotes/author/cecil-baxter.

Belic, R., director. 2011. *Happy*. Wadi Rum Films and Shady
Acres.

Belton, L. W. 2016. *A Nobler Side of Leadership: The Art of
Humanagement: A Servant Leader Journey*. Atlanta,
GA: The Greenleaf Center for Servant Leadership.

Brooks, D. 2019. "The Lies Our Culture Tells Us About What Mat-
ters—and a Better Way to Live." Retrieved March 28,
2021, from https://youtu.be/iB4MS1hsWXU.

Caro, N., director. 2005. *North Country*. United States: Partici-
pant Productions.

Christakis, N. A., and J. H. Fowler. 2009. *Connected: The Sur-
prising Power of Our Social Networks and How They
Shape Our Lives*. New York: Little, Brown Spark.

Dictionary.com. 2021. "Definition of Regenerate Is." Retrieved
March 29, 2021, from https://www.dictionary.com/
browser/regenerate.

Dill, E. 2018. "The Sexual Harassment Class-Action Started at a
Minnesota Mine That Helped Set a National Precedent."
Retrieved February 8, 2021, from https://minnpost.

com/mnopedia/2018/02sexual-harassment-class-action-started-minnesota-mine-helped-set-national-precedent/.

Friedman, T. L. 2016. *Thank You for Being Late: An Optimist's Guide to Thriving in the Age of Accelerations.* New York: Farrar, Straus, and Giroux.

Gilbert, D. 2006. *Stumbling on Happiness.* New York: Vintage Books.

Gladwell, M. 2007. "Choice, Happiness, and Spaghetti Sauce." Retrieved March 25, 2021, from https://youtu.be/iliAAhUeR6Y.

Goodreads, Inc. 2021. Retrieved March 24, 2021, from https://www.goodreads.com/quotes/114729-he-who-fights-and-runs-away-may-live-to-fight#,~text=May%20live20to %20fight%20again.%E2%80%9D.

Greenburg, J. 2012. *Behavior in Organizations,* 10th ed. New Delhi: Prentice-Hall of India Pvt.

Greenleaf, R. K. 1996. *Seeker and Servant: Reflections on Religious Leadership.* San Francisco: Jossey-Bass Publishers.

Greenleaf, R. K. 2002. *Servant Leadership: A Journey into the Nature of Legitimate Power and Greatness.* Mahwah, NJ: Paulist Press.

Heider, J. 1985. *The Tao of Leadership: Lao Tzu's Tao Te Ching Adapted for a New Age.* New York: Sterling Publishing.

Herzberg, F. 2008. *One More Time: How Do You Motivate Employees?* Harvard Business Review Classics. Boston: MA: Harvard Business Review Press.

Jacobs, J. 1992. *Systems of Survival: A Dialog on the Moral Foundations of Commerce and Politics.* New York: Random House.

Kaufman, S.C. N.d. "Self-Actualization Tests." Retrieved March

20, 2020, from https://scottbarykuafman.com/selfac-tualizationtests/.

Kouzes, J. M., and B. Z. Posner. 2011. *Credibility: How Leaders Gain and Lose It, Why People Demand It*. San Francisco: Jossey-Bass.

Marshall, J. M., III. 2009. *The Power of Four: Leadership Lessons from Crazy Horse, Know Yourself, Know Your Friends, Know the Enemy, Lead the Way*. New York: Sterling Publishing.

McCauley, D. P., and K. W. Kuhnert. 1992. "A Theoretical Review and Empirical Investigation of Employee Trust in Management." *Public Administration Quarterly* 16 (2) (Summer 1992): 265–284.

McGuire, T. 2004. "How Can You Make Your Job about More Than Work?" Retrieved March 16, 2004, from http://www.startribune.com/stories/614/4656326. html.

Mintzberg, H. 2013. *Simply Managing: What Managers Do—and Can Do Better*. Oakland, CA: Berrett-Koehler.

Musk, J. 2016. "Wounded People Tell Better Stories." Tedx, San Francisco. Retrieved March 2, 2021, from https://youtu.be/EVGoWvZMFzo on 2-22-2021.

Online Etymology Dictionary. 2021. "Origin and Meaning of Organization." Retrieved March 18, 2021, from https://www.etymonline.com/word/organization.

Osborne, B. 2013. Ethics and the Role of Leadership. Cardinal Stritch University, Milwaukee, WI.

Patrnchak, J. M. 2016. *The Engaged Enterprise: A Field Guide for the Servant-Leader*. Atlanta, GA: The Greenleaf Center for Servant Leadership.

Peterson, J. B. 2018. *12 Rules for Life: An Antidote to Chaos.* Toronto: Random House Canada.

Pucetaite, R., A. Novelskaite, and L. Markunaite. 2015. "The Mediating Role of Leadership Relationship in Building Organizational Trust on Ethical Culture of an Organization." *Economics and Sociology* 8 (3): 11–31. DOI: 10.14254/2071-789x.2015/8-3/1.

Putnam, R. 2000. *Bowling Alone: The Collapse and Revival of American Community.* New York: Simon & Schuster.

Schwartz, B. 2000. *The Costs of Living: How Market Freedom Erodes the Best Things in Life.* New York: W. W Norton.

Semler, R. 2004. *The Seven-Day Weekend: Changing the Way Work Works.* Johannesburg, South Africa: Penguin Group.

Showkeir, J., and M. Showkeir. 2008. *Authentic Conversations: Moving from Manipulation to Truth and Commitment.* Oakland, CA: Berrett-Koehler Publishers.

Spears, L. C. 1998. *Insights on Leadership: Service, Spirit, and Servant Leadership.* New York: John Wiley and Sons.

Whyte, D. 1994. *The Heart Aroused: Poetry and the Preservation of the Soul in Corporate America.* New York: Doubleday.

About the Author

Bernard Osborne obtained his master of servant leadership (MASL) degree from Viterbo University and a bachelor of science in management with a certificate in human resources from Cardinal Stritch University. He is a lifelong employee of the flow-instrumentation side of Badger  Meter. He continues to grow his unique perspective on leadership and management through the real-life challenges and educational programs and activities sponsored by the organization, one of which includes Leadership Racine, where after graduating in 2016, he has been graciously presented with the opportunity to deliver the opening presentation on servant leadership to each new class. He has also introduced and facilitates the servant leadership/followership roundtable for his community.

Volunteer activities include chairing a board seat for Big Brothers Big Sisters, the executive fund-raising committee for the American Heart Association, numerous United Way fund-raising campaigns, and chairing the property and grounds, youth, missions, and vice president positions for the Lutheran Church of the Redeemer church council. He is the founder of the Spirit Root Flute Circle for Native American Flutes (NAF), which is registered with the World Flute Society, and a member of the Healing Earth Flute Circle in Illinois. He also completed a course on Chi-Running and has shared his running experience and knowledge to help new and emerging runners discover the joy of pain-free running. He currently resides in Racine, Wisconsin, with his wife and three rescued shelter dogs. His hobbies are reading and continuous education, playing the NAF, tongue-pan drums, bass guitar, recumbent bike riding, cooking, working in his small native-plant prairie garden, dressing as a mascot for children's birthday parties, and participating in interactive Halloween yard displays.